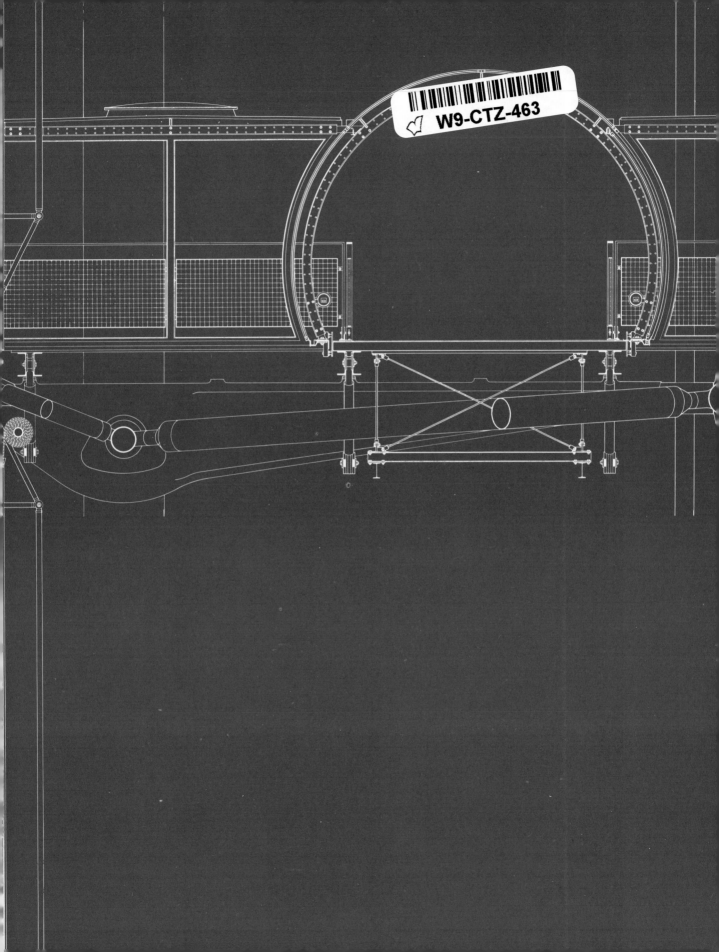

BY THEIR OWN DESIGN

BY THEIR OWN DESIGN

EDITED BY ABBY SUCKLE

WHITNEY LIBRARY OF DESIGN
an imprint of Watson-Guptill Publications/New York

Norman Foster: The description of the Willis Faber Building
is based on an article that appeared in *Architectural Design,*
September-October 1978.

Herman Hertzberger: Appeared originally in Dutch *Forum,* vol. XXIV-3 (1973).

Cesar Pelli: Based on an interview and adapted with permission
from *Architectural Record,* mid-August 1979.

First published 1980 in the United States and Canada by Whitney Library of Design,
an imprint of Watson-Guptill Publications,
a division of Billboard Publications, Inc.,
1515 Broadway, New York, N.Y. 10036

Library of Congress Cataloging in Publication Data
Main entry under title:
By their own design.
    1. Architectural design. 2. Architecture—
Philosophy. I. Suckle, Abby, 1952–
NA2750.B9 1980   721′.092′2   79-28244
ISBN 0-8230-7097-2

Manufactured in U.S.A.

First Printing, 1980

Edited by Sharon Lee Ryder and Susan Davis
Designed by Bob Fillie

A building being built is not yet in servitude. It is so anxious to be that no grass can grow under its feet, so high is the spirit of wanting to be. When it is in service and finished, the building wants to say, "look, I want to tell you about the way I was made." Nobody listens. Everybody is busy going from room to room.

But when the building is a ruin and free of servitude, the spirit emerges telling of the great marvel that a building was made.

LOUIS I. KAHN
quoted in *Architecture + Urbanism*
January 1973

Acknowledgments

Normally in a first book, the fledgling writer composes a rhapsody in prose which heralds the praises of everyone who has had anything to do with the *magnum opus*. Mine is short in part because this is a short book and in part because not very many people were present throughout the two (or more) years that comprise the chronicle that is the history of this book. Mostly they took part in hand-holding and mostly they are former classmates of mine who know absolutely nothing more about architecture (or even sentence structure) than I do and were perfectly willing to have a learning experience. Which made them quite agreeable companions and critics.

The lion's share of the acknowledgments are due to Misako Sammye Akutsu. She has several unique attributes which surpass her ''boy scout'' virtues of being organized, trustworthy, neat, and prepared that turned out to be very valuable. She possesses two Master of Architecture degrees from Harvard (her second is in urban design) as opposed to my one. She is completely fluent in Japanese which is her native language. And most importantly, I was able to cajole her in addition to Franziska Amacher, Jim Treichler, and Chuck Lauster into reading some of the articles at one point or another and making intelligent remarks about them; Peter Arendt provided moral support.

The people who really helped the book evolve from its initial fuzzy conception to its final materialization and taught me more about architecture than I ever learned in school were the contributors. They were uniformly encouraging and patient with me. Some of them devoted so much time to their essays that I secretly wondered how they ever managed to get their own work done. To them I dedicate this book.

CONTENTS

INTRODUCTION

A building has to start in the unmeasurable aura and go through the measurable to be accomplished. It is the only way you can build, the only way that you can get it into being is through the measurable. You must follow the laws, but in the end, when the building becomes part of living it evokes unmeasurable qualities. The design involving quantities of brick, methods of construction and engineering is finished and the spirit of its existence takes over.

Louis I. Kahn

Picture the poor contemporary architect slaving away at his (or her) drawing board, caught between the esoteric *pensees* of *Oppositions* proudly displayed on one side of him and the weighty reality of *Sweet's Catalog* anchoring the other as he struggles to produce the quintessence of postmodern design. All the while he is wondering whether he is Don Quixote jousting at windmills or foreshadowing the artistic trends of the eighties.

Since it tends to be infinitely easier to criticize what other people have designed than to do it yourself, most of the treatises published to date on architectural design are rarely as useful as they could or should be when it comes time for the architect to sit down at his drawing board and actually design. For then he must consciously decide what to communicate to whom, how to do it in the clearest possible way so that it can be read by the intended audience, and how to keep that message from being drowned by the torrent of constraints that inevitably accompany the building process.

Concerned with questions of design, construction, and architecture, this book reveals the various ways in which ten architects synthesize the first and the second into the third. It is a book about values that architects hold about how people should live and interact, about community and privacy, about art and technology. It is a book about the many things that inspire a design, which range from the pragmatic conditions of a program to idealized prototypical solutions that can be built anywhere at anytime; from sociological notions about how people should use their surroundings to sculptural compositions that present abstracted spatial concepts. It is a book about meaning and what sort of messages can and cannot be conveyed in a building. It is a book about the process of design, about the marriage of aesthetic concerns with structural ones. It is a book about where the architect chooses to lavish his finite amount of tender loving care as well as where the money is spent. And mostly it is a book about the architect as master builder, the person who coordinates all the many people involved in the building process and makes all the critical decisions.

Each of the ten architects who contributed an essay is very much a master builder. Each has a strong design philosophy. Each cares a lot about how his buildings are resolved technically. Each has a philosophy of construction, a framework of interlocking values and viewpoints which form a coherent set of principles involved in directing the formal properties of build, of materials, and of their connections to each other.

Some of the architects, for example, narrowly define the scope of architecture as construction and choose to express the actual making of the building as Richard Rogers does in Plateau Beauborg, where every part is differentiated, defined, and assembled as an erector set in such a way that the process of construction is easily perceived and understood. Others, such as John Johansen, also split buildings into their component parts; those which are more temporary are clipped onto those which are more permanent in an attempt to deal with growth and change. Both architects also prefer to build in steel. But Johansen's work, such as the Mummers Theater, is characterized more by its ad hoc approach to detailing, overlaid with an electrical circuit imagery and a sculptural sensitivity, than by a highly rational approach to construction.

Some architects, like Harry Seidler, believe in

using the building's structure as the primary ordering device and express it as such; they weave the other elements through that in a logical way. A building such as the Australian Embassy in Paris shares with Arthur Erickson's Museum of Ethnology in Vancouver a concrete construction and expression, where the structure defines highly sculptural spaces. Both architects view construction as architecture with a capital A, and both like to generate forms in a primarily sculptural fashion. The difference is that Erickson even candidly admits to giving structure a back seat to consideration of other issues, from siting and aesthetics to user response, while Seidler lets structure predominate over these other concerns.

Another approach is the one that Norman Foster takes; he chooses to minimize visual clutter and refine away the redundant, unnecessary, inefficient parts of the building. This involves searching for the most appropriate technology and rethinking the way that we commonly approach construction. It is also interwoven with a brand of sociological utopianism that Herman Hertzberger might be sympathetic to. One need only compare the virtually identical programs of Foster's Willis Faber Building and Hertzberger's Centraal Beheer: both insurance companies relocating in a suburban town about two hours away from their capital cities, both plagued with employee attrition, and both desiring to make life in the suburbs attractive for their 1,500 workers. While Foster refines away all the extraneous elements, Hertzberger goes to considerable trouble to incorporate as many as he can conceive of into his scheme. By constructing small-scale forms, concrete block nooks and crannies that double as storage units and space dividers, handrails that are also benches, he provides the users of his buildings with elements they can appropriate as their own.

Both Kisho Kurokawa and Fumihiko Maki are seeking ways to combine a cultural tradition with the vocabulary of modern architecture. While they have both been Metabolists and both been interested in growth and change, Kurokawa is much more interested in the meanings of architecture which are not restricted to rationality, which can relate to Buddhist philosophy, and which are much more difficult to build and infinitely more complicated to read. His architecture veers in the direction of systemized building—of plugging capsules into a supporting core, as in the Nakagin Capsule Tower. Maki's work is much more pragmatic, much more straightforward. He is looking for an appropriate scale for industrialized construction so that it can be an identifiable building module for design at the same time that the module can vary slightly in design to reflect the programmatic variations of the building.

Another way of looking at architecture is as a strictly pragmatic endeavor where the architect tries to synthesize the programmatic requirements into a whole which, as the cliche goes, is more than the sum of the parts. Both Gerald McCue and Cesar Pelli exemplify this almost traditional view of the architect. Both have done many buildings for large corporate clients. Here again, there are fundamental differences, for McCue is interested in a logical conceptual model for his approach to construction so that it is conceptually consistent within each building. Pelli is more concerned with aesthetics. He believes in ready-made, available materials, and his artistic expression is derived from the constraints of the program. McCue's IBM Headquarters is like much of Pelli's work in many respects. It has a slick panelized skin which is painted bright colors. But it is not nearly as molded a form or as instantly imageable as the extruded blue section of the Pacific Design Center.

What characterizes these ten viewpoints is that they run the gamut of design stances. What each architect does is present his own design philosophy and show how it is resolved in one or more recent buildings. This book shows only how divergent the possibilities for shaping buildings are. It does not and cannot offer any definitive conclusions for how design is to be done.

ARTHUR ERIKSON

Arthur Erickson received his Bachelor of Architecture from McGill University in 1950. He also won a traveling scholarship which enabled him to tour the continent, particularly Greece, Italy, and northern Europe. On his return he taught first at the University of Oregon and then at the University of British Columbia, where he became an associate professor in 1961. During this time he maintained a small private practice building mostly houses. He then received a fellowship to go to Japan and made the first of many trips to the Orient. In 1963, in partnership with Geoffrey/Massey, he received the first prize in the competition for Simon Fraser University for an innovative scheme featuring a quarter-mile-long, glass-covered central mall surrounded by low-profile concrete classroom and laboratory buildings. When completed two years and $20 million later, it was considered by many to be one of the best of the new campuses of the sixties.

Since then Erickson has built widely. His work varies from an egg crate-like shelter built out of laminated recycled newspapers by the schoolchildren of Vancouver for the UN Habitat Conference, to the Canadian pavilion at Expo '70, an intricate play of mirrored surfaces, to the recent courthouse/redevelopment scheme for the center of Vancouver, which is now completed. He has received numerous awards, including the Tau Sigma Delta Gold Medal of the American Institute of Architects and the Auguste Perret Award of the International Union of Architects. He has also been the recipient of several honorary degrees from such institutions as the University of Manitoba and McGill. Since his approach to architecture is primarily a sculptural one, it will be interesting to see finished the new concert hall he is working on in Toronto, which sports a steel net roof supporting panels of mirror glass.

Inside the great hall of the Museum of Anthropology at the University of British Columbia are the magnificently carved totem poles of the Northwest Coast Indians. The roof is supported by the small beams running across the space, not by the deep beams.

The structural specialist meets the demands of pure structure alone. His art has progressed through the interaction of the strength of materials and the physics of forces to produce bridges of lissome beauty, crystalline domes, majestic dams, and brave structures of awesome spans. It is a discipline whose parameters are clear: how, with the least material and minimum effort, the heroic feats of force and span can be accomplished.

Structural Expression in Architecture: An Historical Overview

But that was never the choice of architecture. In recent years, the role of structure has become more confused since architects themselves, intimidated by the bravura of the structural specialists and under pressure from the public gallery to do equally spectacular tricks, have tried to justify their work in structural terms. Techtonics, in fact, have so dominated our priorities and overwhelmed less tangible values, such as the traditional desire to bring a building into harmony with the cosmos by means of geometric proportion and orientation and to implant it with anthropomorphic symbolism, that in the last century we have reevaluated history as man's progress in materials and techtonics. Examples abound. They range from Viollet le Duc's attempt to redefine Gothic architecture in terms of medieval rationalism to the scientific rational approach of some of the most avant garde schools in the early part of the century, which scarcely bothered to teach history at all. We overlooked or conveniently forgot the fact that concrete had been around for several thousand years, that the arch and vault were in use long before the Romans, just as gunpowder and electricity had been known in ancient China, but used only as a source of amusement.

Looking at the historical record, it seems that innovation in itself was not as significant in human progress as the use to which that innovation is put. Thus our historians have mistakenly argued that the Gothic arch was an innovation in technique that brought forth a new exploration of the enclosure of spaces—but it was not. Instead it was a fashion brought back from the Crusades: the returning Normans introduced the already-ancient Saracenic arch into Europe as a decorative motif. It was taste, fashion, and the suitability of the form to the aspirations of the time that decreed its influence. Only incidental to that and much later was its structural potential realized. Structurally,

in fact, the Gothic arch was an afterthought in that its structural possibilities were thought about subsequent to its aesthetic ones. As an unbiased look at history will prove, not until this last century was there much concern at all for structural technique in the development of the styles. Before this, it was not an isolated discipline with its own intellectual terms of reference as it is now. Rather it was an unconscious tradition in building method that evolved through decades, even centuries, of collective experience. Techtonics were merely a means to achieve far more important goals in the interest of architecture as a whole.

For the Greeks who were the greatest of artists, structure was wisely of the least importance. Their Doric temples are constructed on a post-and-lintel structural system borrowed from early timber prototypes, a structure which is difficult to build in stone. For the Romans, who were the first real technicians, ingenuity in structure was such a source of embarrassment that they carefully hid masterful brick vaulting under a veneer of Greek trabeation. A Greek portico marks the entry to the Pantheon; its concrete dome spanning 141 feet (43 meters) was the largest clearspan structure for nearly 2,000 years. Much later in the Renaissance and Baroque periods, builders never bothered to surpass by much the structural mastery of the Romans, as they were primarily concerned with the rediscovery and celebration of earthly physicality, an anthropocentric conception of the world which viewed man's body as divine and felt that his proportions and physical attributes should be reflected in architecture. Later builders became caught up in the excitement of shaping new spaces, featuring floodlit interiors topped with illusionistic murals, stately staircases, and highly organized arrangements of rooms. It was only with the subsequent advent of Western industrialism and its consequent division of labor resulting in the specialization of knowledge, experience, and discipline that structure became an end in itself, and a kind of structuralism began to influence our thought.

The Structural Aesthetic

Following the influence of the first engineers at the great 19th-century expositions, it was only in our time that a structural aesthetic began to assert itself in architectural style. At the beginning of the century the Russian constructivists with the sculptures, for instance, of Gabo or Tatlin's Monument to the Third International, the Italian futurists with the drawings of Sant'Elia, and the Dutch purists with the work of Rietvelt, Oud, and

the furniture of Van Doesburg reflected the new preoccupation with the aesthetic of structure. The Bauhaus, which was to move from Weimer and Dessau to America where innovation was a clearly frenetic pursuit, was to institutionalize it for good. The machine aesthetic celebrated by Mies and Corbusier still haunts us to the extent that even today at the very forefront of design the method of doing is more important than what is done. If it had not been for such miscreants as Wright, who wholesomely avoided that whole aesthetic trough, we might have lost the thread of architecture altogether. Today, having nearly reached the sterile end of that mechanistic pursuit, we sense that maybe the threads of architecture in its broadest human sense are about to be picked up again.

If one looks at the catalog of contemporary buildings, it is obvious that those of a predominantly structural bias are not, in the total sense, architecture. By illustration one can observe the buildings of Nervi where the dichotomy is clearest. No one questions the sheer aesthetic beauty of his structures—the bridges, the domes, the hangars—but one would expect that degree of structural taste and refinement from an engineer who is also Italian, because of the long history of Italian aesthetic sensitivity. However, on examination of his buildings, the flaws appear in all those aspects where the functions do not mandate a large span, the aspects that have to do with the human occupation of these structures. The walls, partitions, doors, windows, handrails are unresolved, awkward, and not integral to the total scheme of the building—and a building falls short of architecture if it is not such a totality. The problem stems from the fact that a structural engineer rightfully thinks only of structure—that is his justification after all. If it is a dome, he is only concerned with the system of spanning that dome, how one enters or partitions or furnishes it is quite secondary, and Fuller's domes bear witness to that. Concentrating exclusively on one aspect of the program such as structure is a simplistic attitude which is not valid since there are a multiplicity of concerns to be answered.

Architecture is so much more complex. Not only must it answer questions of purpose, site, suitable spaces, technical systems, and materials in a totally integrated way, but it must be appropriately significant and meaningful in its physical and social context to those who use or observe it. Therefore, the structure is only one aspect of a more subtle and diverse whole—no more or less significant than the human skeletal frame is to the total of a thinking and feeling person. When all factors are balanced in architecture, no one aspect of a building stands out as unique, more important, or separate from the whole. If on seeing a building the response is "what an interesting

Top: At the Museum of An-
thropology the concrete piers
and channels of the great hall
range from low wide spans of
120 feet (36 meters) to tall
narrow spans of only 40 feet
(12 meters), yet the channels
are consistently as deep as the
piers are wide.

Bottom: Facing the shore of
an artificial lake, the concrete
channels and piers of the
great hall metaphorically recall the longhouse frames
housed within, which were
also built on the beaches.

structure," something is wrong. Henceforth the structure can be remembered, but the building forgotten.

Structural Ambiguity

Contrary to most contemporary theories of architecture, perhaps, my opinion is that on observation a building should not reveal immediately how it is built. That aspect should only be obvious after study and in the end seem quite sensible, but not necessarily that logical. The open space grids of Mies and Corbu, for instance, are in retrospect both architectural and structural copouts as they do not respond directly to the particular spatial requirements and have little to do with the genius of their architecture. Logic after all is the enemy of art.

But as with so many of my generation, I had to go through the indoctrination of the priority of structure over all other considerations. We were trained to draw structural grids, to put in columns, and then to draw a building around the columns. Such a mechanistic approach to architecture may still persist in some schools of architecture, and I pity the students who must endure it, for it took me long enough to recover from the deception that it was the most appropriate methodology for design. But now I feel fully confident in being independent of the structural crutch and illogical about structure; this shows in my best buildings.

That does not mean that a building should not have a structural veracity, just as any individual must have a structural veracity in order to move about. Since a building is to a degree a structure, it must be resolved and expressed as such. For me, though, this is an aesthetic view: a building needs to have a strong structural presence. But the structure, rather than being the first, should and must be the last aspect to be considered in the evolution of a building.

Structure is the strongest and most powerful element of form, so much so that if it is not the last consideration in the long series of decisions determining form, it distorts or modifies all other important determinates of a building. One finds, in fact, that the structure has dictated all the other aspects of the design. The inhabitants should not behave as the columns dictate—the contrary should surely be the case.

Museum of Anthropology

An example of my approach to structure is the recently completed Museum of Anthropology at the University of British Columbia in Vancouver.

There perhaps could not be a better case of structural ambiguity: the structure is not the most efficient or optimal to support the space and it doesn't work as it appears to. But it works superbly for what it is and has a strong and unforgettable structural impact. As with all my buildings the structure was not even considered until the main premises of the design—the shape of the spaces and the form of the building—had been determined. Thus, the structure did not preclude but followed the design intent.

The design stemmed from several issues: the need to house a superb collection of Northwest Coast native art, including an imposing group of Haida and Kwakiutl massive carvings, some up to 45 feet (14 meters) in height; the need to be a teaching museum for a collection of other aboriginal cultures; the potential of an inspiring cliffside site overlooking the inlets of the British Columbia seacoast; the existence on the site of some World War II gun emplacements which would have to be incorporated in the museum; and the severe limitations of budget.

The design evolved out of the determination to use the site, gun emplacements and all, to the maximum advantage and began more as a landscape concept than an architectural one. The sea view offered the opportunity to recreate outside the museum the true Northwest Coast village seaside setting. A body of water placed at the cliff edge and visually merging with the sea below could, with poles and long houses set on its banks, give the illusion of the typical native village on a coastal inlet.

With this idea established, a model of the site was built: then the poles and house frames as well as the poles to be housed inside the museum were mocked up and placed on the site model. The order of viewing the poles in the museum could be established from the model, and in turn, the kind and sequence of spaces enclosing them could be determined, proceeding from the entrance lobby down the slope to the great exhibition hall containing the massive carvings. The existing gun emplacements on the site produced a tight constriction in the series of spaces, their curved forms easing the transition from the introductory rooms to the great hall. The other elements of the building—the exhibition, storage, work, and administrative spaces, not of significance here—fell into place around the spine of spaces thus created. Only after this had been laid out, the spaces articulated, and the size and height of the building determined was there any consideration of how to "structure" these spaces—in particular the long spans of the great hall. The peculiar shape of the great hall bursting outwards to the lake and distant

view was determined by the height of the poles and the desire for them to be viewed in a natural light against a natural setting with as unprepossessing a background as possible.

I have long preferred in spite of structural inefficiency, the visual ambiguity of columns and beams being the same size. Logically the beams should be narrow and deep for bending moments and the columns in compression proportionately smaller. But this makes for a great deal of visual tension. The appeal of uniform size is best shown in my early Smith House where the lack of the expected visual tension between column and beam (because both were cut out of the same timber) gave the structure a great visual repose. So in the great hall of the museum, a simple column and precast channel system, both of the same width and section, was chosen, though the columns were single piers instead of channels. But the discipline imposed upon the structural solution was that whatever the span of the channel, which varied from 40 to 120 feet (12 to 36 meters), or the height of the pier, which varied from 15 to 45 feet (4.5 to 14 meters)—whatever the variation in stresses—I did not want to show it. Rather, I wanted the structure to appear as a uniform backdrop for the display. There is, therefore, enormous redundancy in the structure proposed; the structure in fact does not even work the way it seems to. Instead of spanning the space as they appear to do, most of the channels hang in the space. The real structural members are the almost invisible sloping beams which seem to be spaces between the channels. It was the ingenuity of my very skillful and patient engineer, Bogaslav Babicki, who made sense out of my whim.

I have been questioned by students as to why I did not resort to a lighter column system—an open steel space frame for the walls, for instance—more in keeping with the expressed desire to open the great hall to the natural surroundings. But such schemes would have introduced a pattern disturbing, in my view, to the visual quiet necessary for the contemplation of the massive carvings. I wanted the wide blank surfaces of the concrete piers to show off by their very blandness the exquisite and subtle relief of the weathered gray carvings of the Haida and the more dramatic carvings of the Kwakiutl. There is a monumental gravity to those carvings that would not be complimented by too thin, nervous, or highly patterned a structure. They required a weightier rhythm—a quietness of line and surface that would seem beyond time and fashion and outside of history as they themselves seem to be.

The frames formed by channel and pier bear an uncanny resemblance to the aboriginal house frame, abstracted and repeated as a sequence of portals, which contributes to the ritualistic feeling of the great hall. It is not just the space, but the massive carvings, the space, the structure, and the setting which combine to achieve this effect. The structure is forceful, but not more than the space, nor the space more than the objects shown therein.

Structure as Afterthink

How can one isolate structure and its logic from such subjective considerations as these that are fundamental to design? Such intangible concerns are almost beyond the scope of analysis and stem from the unconscious levels of the mind—surely a far richer resource than conscious thought. Structure must take its directions from there as well. That is the difference between pure structure and architecture. When structure is influenced by other factors of a building and a space, it cannot retain its purity. By definition it must be subject to other, nonstructural determinates to function as architecture and act as a totality.

Through familiarization with the building's intent, the design evolves out of the complexity of the myriad considerations that the building must resolve. It is perhaps not structure as afterthought, for the process is too cohesive for any part of it to occur after the fact, but it is structure that emerges only as the final tailoring of the forms which have emerged in the process. Structure makes the formal idea buildable as the form itself must in the end be structural.

Thus may we try to bury finally and irrevocably the notion of structure as a predeterminant of form. So also must we abolish the idea of a logic to the design process or of an order of priority to the considerations that enter a design. To consciously decide that the site, the climate, the use, or techniques should have priority is to eliminate the possibility of some unannounced or unpremeditated aspect offering the motivation for design. In the process of conceptualizing a design, all aspects of a project have to be viewed equally without bias or prejudgment. The deeper and broader the scan of the subject and the wider the intake of factors impinging even remotely on it, the more pertinent the solution will be. Structure alone cannot be the subject of that scanning process unless the project is predominantly structural, for structure has to do with the final stage of realization, the actual construction. It is only then, when the idea is fully rounded and flushed out, that structure should come into play and bring its discipline to give shape and substance to the amorphic form. In that sense it is afterthink.

Top: The concrete channels and piers of the Museum of Anthropology entry hall reflect not only the Indian longhouse frames, but relate to the framing of the great hall.

Bottom: While the concrete channels appear to be supporting the roof of the great hall, the nearly invisible cross members are actually doing the work.

CESAR PELLI

Born in Tucuman, Argentina, in 1926, Cesar Pelli received his architectural degree from the university there. He came to the United States to study at the University of Illinois in 1952 on a scholarship from the Institute of International Education. Shortly after receiving his Masters, he joined Eero Saarinen's office where he worked on such buildings as the TWA terminal at Kennedy Airport and the Vivian Beaumont Theater at Lincoln Center in New York, for which he was the project designer. Pelli collaborated with such designers as Gunnar Birkerts, Paul Kennon, Tony Lumsden, Warren Platner, and Kevin Roche in the Saarinen office during his ten years there.

When Saarinen died, Pelli left the firm to become director of design at Daniel, Mann, Johnson, and Mendenhall, a large corporate architecture/engineering firm in Los Angeles. He received a Progressive Architecture design award for a projected urban nucleus in the Santa Monica mountains. Two other buildings designed during this period—COMSAT Laboratories and Teledyne Systems—are notable for their linear organizations along a pedestrian street allowing for growth and change which form the organizational principle for his later award-winning scheme for the United Nations Headquarters and conference center in Vienna.

This building was one of the first projects executed after he moved to Gruen Associates as the partner in charge of design. While at Gruen, he also designed the Commons and Courthouse Center in Columbus, Indiana. Perhaps the first building of its type, it functions as the town center, combining shopping and community facilities within one building. He was also responsible for the design of the U.S. Embassy in Tokyo.

Currently he is engaged in the design of the galley expansion and condominium tower of the Museum of Modern Art, several housing projects, an office building, and his first single family house. In these projects, the use of spandrel glass, which he has pioneered as a very economical cladding system, has been refined to the point where he is treating it as a mosaic in colors, much like a Mondrian.

Pelli has also been teaching consistently since 1960, first at UCLA, then as a visiting professor and critic at Yale, and since 1976 as its dean. He has published articles in A + U, Progressive Architecture, *and* Architectural Record.

The escalator well at the Pacific Design Center is treated as a sculptural element attached to the mass of the building.

Technology is only one element that architecture deals with, but it is inescapable. Buildings have to be built with something, and building technology is simply the way in which materials are used and labor is organized. There is always a point where we must consider the relationship between design intentions and the reality of building, and it is my contention that in any healthy architecture these two things cannot be far apart.

From the inception of the modern movement, many architects were totally uninterested in historical issues because those issues did not help their thinking or contribute to the way they resolved buildings. One of the basic tenets of the modern movement was that regardless of what you designed, it had to be closely related to the way it was built. Even more than that, you had to make a point of it. Today; some architects in the modern tradition are still looking for a technology that will symbolically appear progressive and modern, a symbol of a new architecture for a new era. But by comparison with other areas of technological development, there is really no "high technology" in architecture. In the latter part of the 20th century, high technology is what scientists use to send Voyager and Mariner into space. In architecture we have nothing more than an expression of high technology used for artistic purposes.

We are now going through a period when ideas and the consensus within the architectural profession are shifting rapidly. Certain attitudes toward design that were vigorous ten years ago no longer exist. Many people who were working in the midst of the stream have suddenly been left high and dry. Some architects may survive to find themselves again in the stream, but for many the current will move away.

Right now we are dealing with several coexisting aesthetic systems. Aesthetic systems tend to get defined as a framework and architects establish their own particular standards within them: what's good, what's bad, what's better than the other. But once the yardstick of one system is used to measure another aesthetic system, the architects working in the first system will, by definition, be dreadful in the second because they will not measure up at all. For example, you cannot judge the architecture of a Norman Foster or a Michael Graves at the same time with the same yardstick. One or the other will appear to be a bad architect.

You can do architecture that depends on a system of proportions, or on a relationship to human beings, or on historical traditions. And with any of these if you are good, you can end up with a work of art.

Technological Expression

I think that architects work within the context that happens to coincide with their own particular interests and ways of searching. Some architects are working at the edge, pushing. Some may be pushing for the maximum recollection of history, some for the maximum expression of industrialized materials. But these efforts are really at the edge. The edges are always the silhouette; they immediately become noticed.

But you don't need to make an architecture that represents the past. And you don't need to make an architecture that represents the future. Neither of these two positions deals with the reality of getting buildings built today. They are both idealized tendencies that have been fighting with each other. Those architects will go farthest whose efforts are reinforced by the ideas of the present.

I believe that a healthy architecture should represent today—should deal with the technology of today—and the technology of today is industrialized. But not all *that* industrialized.

Such a position can be seen in the problem of designing and building a house where the most developed technology is wood frame construction. It is the most economical, the most available, the most developed, and the one that will allow you to have the greatest number of aesthetic choices. In New England, you would use clapboards or shingles; in Southern California, chicken wire and stucco. Those would be the most appropriate technologies and you would get the best results for the least money. This is what labor knows how to build. This is what we interpret as a house today and what future buyers will want from a house. And it will be more adaptable to additions and alterations.

If you are doing a highrise office building, you really cannot talk of anything except concrete or steel structure, and some sort of enclosure that will not be structural, but will probably be a curtain wall. How you use this for an artistic expression is another issue.

You cannot build a building that does not conform to codes and government regulations. You cannot pretend that there are no labor unions. You cannot pretend that there is still a high level of craftsmanship. Those facts are pragmatic and real.

One has to make architecture with the things that are available: with the technology that is available, with the social system that is available,

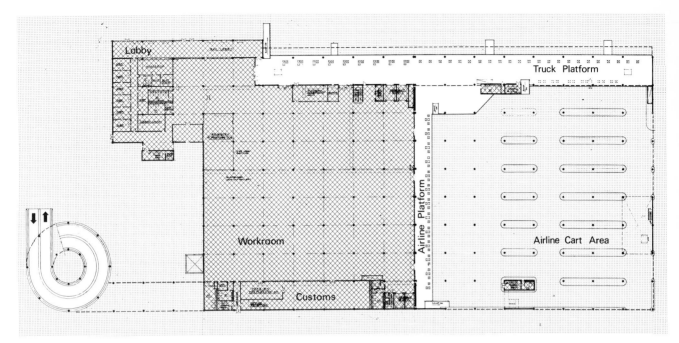

with the economics that is available. That's the only architecture which allows the development of forms that can be carried on by other architects and which other generations can develop and transform. They can continue relating to what is really there.

Worldway Postal Center

The Worldway Postal Center at the Los Angeles Airport is an international mail handling facility, the first fully mechanized post office to be located at a major U.S. airport. Post office officials had a very clear idea of what they wanted and gave us what virtually amounted to a design of the building. While many architects receiving this kind of design package would spend a lot of time redefining and redesigning it, we didn't. Since their requests and recommendations seemed to be appropriate to their needs we took their plan and built it with a few minor modifications.

We designed a tough, industrial building with no frills. We wanted it hard and tight. I mean physically hard, like brick and concrete, to take a good deal of rough use through many years, and tight, with no projections or added elements.

The Post Office Department wanted round concrete columns with conical capitals to support floors of flat slab construction. They prefer this structural system because holes can be cut at almost any point in the slab and a number of ele-

ments like conveyor belts, catwalks, or ducts can be suspended from it in a similarly random manner. At the Worldway Postal Center we exposed the round columns on the exterior. We set panels of brown brick between the columns and cut the capitals flush with the exterior surface of the wall, exposing a parabolic knuckle of concrete at the joint of the column and floor, which looked very much like a Romanesque capital.

This simple action transformed the utilitarian structure into an element of great beauty that gave order and form to the whole project.

Pacific Design Center

Equally pragmatic were the bases for the 1971 design for the Pacific Design Center in Los Angeles. We developed the program for the 13 acres of interior design showrooms and ancillary retail facilities that the building houses along with our developer client. The bulk of the building was derived from two constraints. One was the desire to put all the parking for the building on the ground. The other was to keep the building as low as possible because showrooms on the upper floors tend to receive less traffic. For this reason, we have aligned showrooms on the top two floors along a central galleria space which is capped by a 60-foot (18-meter) high barrel vault, glazed on the north side.

Since our client was interested in spending as little money as possible and since we were interested in varying the perimeter, roof profile, and

The functions of the Worldway Postal Center are allocated within the rigors of the structural grid, as can be seen from this ground floor plan.

Opposite page: In the front elevation of the Worldway Postal Center the hybrid quality of the frame and skin building is readily apparent.

Top: Within this highly structured grid an incredible variety of different functions and cladding materials are infilled while still maintaining a taut facade.

Bottom, left: The ramp to the employee parking on the roof is split from the building by two bays.

Bottom, right: Detail of the recessed column showing the cut mushroom capital and the flush brick and louvers.

interior plan, we searched for an appropriate structural system. A uniform 30-foot (9-meter) square steel column grid proved to be the most economical, efficient, and buildable structure. It was simple and straightforward.

One of the most economical facades for a building of this type is a continuous glass skin. Since there was very little need for clear glass windows, we were able to use spandrel panels of glass, spraypainted with a ceramic grit and then oven baked. A layer of insulation was added to the inside surface of the spandrel, making the facade fairly energy efficient.

Unlike stone glass is a fragile material. It embodies a changing, impermanent, and finite architecture suitable for the functions we house today. The transparency, reflectivity, and perceptual qualities of the material are enhanced by treating it like a skin, as a positive element and not a void. By wrapping the glazing envelope tightly around the building masses, we enhanced the crystalline nature of the extruded form. By very lightly gridding the skin, we were able to hold the surface planes without losing the fragile quality of the material. The neoprene mullions that zipper the pieces of glass together are very flush against the surface and protrude only ⅜ inch (9.5 millimeters) from the skin.

This is one of the aesthetic decisions upon which the strength of the building rests. The other was to make it very blue. Because the spandrel glass is cladding and not windows, we felt that it should have a definite color. We had chosen blue to reflect the blue of the sky. The client had some doubts about that color and wondered if there weren't alternatives. So we presented about ten, ranging from white to very dark colors, saturated to unsaturated. We made a very systematic study, covering a model in different color papers. The yellows looked terrible; the greens were awful; in a pastel shade, the building lost its form. So we ended up recommending only two colors: the blue and a dark desaturated red. We presented the alternatives knowing that when the decision was made, we could go along with the client's choice.

When the blue was chosen, we prepared about twenty large Plexiglas panels with different shades of blue ranging from gray to red blue and more or less saturated. The present blue was selected over the lighter shades which have very little reflection and much less contrast.

The choice of blue and the building's graphically strong profile were an attempt to give the building a personality, an image. All buildings have images. Traditionally architects have been conscious of all the aesthetic impressions, associ-

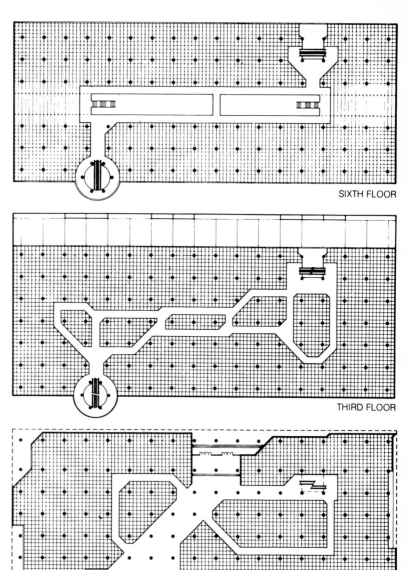

SIXTH FLOOR

THIRD FLOOR

GROUND FLOOR

Opposite page: Looking through the skin of the facade into the guts of the Worldway Postal Center: the loading dock and airline cart area.

Above: Plans showing the variety of corridors at the Pacific Design Center.

Above: The massing of the Pacific Design Center responds directly to programmatic variations within. Superimposed upon them are aesthetic notions. The barrel vault, for instance, is supported by a haunched beam on one side, not because it is structurally advantageous but because we wanted an asymmetrical profile.

Opposite page: Inside the galleria on the sixth floor: in addition to its programmed functions this space has played host to events ranging from fashion shows to weddings.

ations, and moods that a building evokes. I tend to think about it very early in the design process (although not quite at the beginning). By making the large mass of the Design Center completely distinct from its surroundings, it enhances the scale of the surrounding buildings. It is like looking down a street in a port city: you see an ocean liner which is enormous in scale, but which doesn't change the scale of the little buildings around it.

The building has had a decided effect on the community. Other buildings in the previously depressed area are being spruced up; some are even painted blue. Movies have been made there. Pilots on Pacific Southwest Airways even point out the building as they fly overhead. The building is fully rented. Its concentration of design showrooms has made the area even more of a design center than before.

If the color of blue was not a given, neither was the extruded profile. They were opportunities that were perceived and developed, artistic possibilities completely attuned to the technological realities. Blue doesn't cost any more than another color. There is no additional skilled labor required to make it or to install it. Decisions like these—which take advantage of working with the grain of how the building will be made rather than against

it—are for me the appropriate way to use technology. And the appropriate way to make art in architecture.

A long taut wall has great beauty. The Crystal Palace did not depend on the correct proportions of its doors or its relationship to historical elements. It depended on immensity, on sheer vigor, on newness, on the extraordinary light running across the top. That building could have been a hundred feet longer and it would have made no difference. At the Pacific Design Center, the impact likewise depends on the long expanse of the tight blue wall. That becomes very beautiful in itself.

It amused me to find that other architects who visited the building found different aesthetic intentions in it. O.M. Ungers felt that its strength came from the continuity of the grid wrapping over and around the building. Giancarlo de Carlo saw it as a series of interior spaces. Most other architects see it as a statement on scale and color. We all do not respond to a work of art in the same way, and a building is much more than a work of art.

Art in architecture and the beauty of the building come from pushing, with sensitivity, a particular quality to its limit.

Top: Under construction, the fragility of the Pacific Design Center's cladding is most apparent.

Bottom: During the latter phase of construction when the cladding is almost complete, the facade begins to acquire some of the fragile perceptual qualities of glass.

KISHO KUROKAWA

In 1960 at the age of 26, Kisho Kurokawa stepped onto the international stage as a coorganizer of the World Design Conference and a member of the Metabolism group. That group was formed as a way of trying to marry traditional Japanese design with modern architecture so as to accommodate growth and change. At that time he had completed his undergraduate degree at Kyoto University and graduate work in architecture at Tokyo University.

Most of his early projects were proposals for new forms of urban living, and they remained in project form. Typical was his Agricultural City of 1960, a framework of streets into which are fitted a checkerboard of communities all on the second level, freeing the ground for agricultural use. His ideas about architecture of the street were first realized two years later in the Nishijin Labor Center where a series of welfare offices were aligned along a pedestrian circulation spine. Since then he has built more than 35 buildings, numbering among them facilities as diverse as a drive-in restaurant, which is infilled into a megastructural space frame; several pavilions for Expo '70 in Osaka, such as the Toshiba IHI Pavilion, a motion picture pavilion with an amphitheater that rose up and down; and several new towns and government centers throughout the world.

He has published widely, writing 22 books on subjects ranging from prefabricated houses to action architecture. His diverse activities include running a think tank, the Institute for Social Engineering, and a monthly television show.

To establish continuity with the city, indoor furniture at the Fukuoka Bank has been brought outside into the plaza.

belong to the fourth generation of modern architects in Japan. The first, ushered in by the Meiji Restoration of 1867, responded to efforts to raise the curtain shrouding Japan by welcoming the architectural styles of the West with open arms. Reacting to the ensuing proliferation of Baroque banks and Renaissance offices, the second generation infused its buildings with traditional, highly nationalistic Japanese styles. These were then exported to the Asia that Japan was busily colonizing, a chapter abruptly terminated by her defeat in 1945. The post-war period was characterized by the introduction of the work of Le Corbusier and CIAM by such third generation luminaries as Kunio Maekawa and Kenzo Tange. But it was up to my generation, those of us who began building in the late fifties, to synthesize the best of both worlds—the quintessence of our Japanese cultural history and the more pragmatic functionally rational modern architecture.

The Japanese Tradition of Wood Architecture

The Metabolism that we first proposed 20 years ago at the World Design Conference in Tokyo is neither a form nor a style. Rather it is an attempt to create a character for Japanese design responding to our particular social and cultural history, a history rooted in the fact that we build in wood and have always done so. In contrast with the willful monumentality of the stone-based architecture of the West, a wood architecture is temporary, since wood rots and is subject to the whims of the elements. Since we are faced with the inevitable mortality of all our constructions, the physical form becomes only the intermediary conveying the poetic essence of nature. Every other decade, for instance, in a ritual that has been repeated for centuries, the ancient wood Shinto shrines have been replaced with exact replicas. Man-made things are looked upon as an extension of nature; they are frequently left unfinished to afford the user the pleasure of completing the beauty created by the artist. This Japanese philosophy of continuity among architecture, society, and nature has inspired me to develop a concept of the intermediary space, the space between (in Japanese, *engawa* or *en-space*), which is an empty space viewed positively. Translated into built form, it becomes a semipublic space, circumventing the schizophrenic duality, or inside/outside of the West. Traditionally, these spaces are found in Japanese streets, which merge nature outside with private living accommodation within.

An example of this continuity is the covered outdoor plaza of the Fukuoka Bank—a building containing banking headquarters, ancillary offices, a banking hall, and an auditorium—which serves as the mediator interweaving what is internal with what is external in a way that hopefully enriches the quality of human experience. To preserve the continuity of the order of the city, the cornice lines of the surrounding buildings were maintained. The continuity of the environment was also reflected in the ambiguity of what is public and what is private. Street furniture is carried inside. So are the reflecting pools and greenery symbolic of nature. The interior corridors and waiting lounges front onto the plaza below, letting the whole building act as an external passage through the city. The exterior membrane itself was conceived as a tenuous boundary, the thinnest possible barrier to light (a characteristic admittedly in conflict with the issue of privacy). Uniformly clad in a shadowy-gray Angola granite skin, the monolithic walls evoke an impression of in-betweenness and scalelessness. For the windows, I turned to a heat-absorbing, semitransparent glass, which, unfortunately, effectively spoils the sense of vague boundary and interpenetration I struggled to achieve.

The Buddhist Tradition

This conception of continuity springs from the undercurrent of Buddhist thought pervading Japanese culture. Architecture is hardly immune from its profound spiritual and philosophical grip; nor, for that matter, should it be. Buddhism influences the way we perceive and compose space and the kinds of relationships we establish between nature and architecture and between technology and humanity. Nature is viewed as one continuous living process, with death but a part of it; it is considered noble to fulfill one's life and pass away beautifully. This means that human beings should not become too attached to any one particular place or idea, but should be aware of being in eternal time, a part of a greater life transcending time and space. Perhaps this qualifies us as the true inventors of the ecology movement. It also leads to the principle that architecture should change with time, with its attendant ideas about replaceability and interchangeability.

The issue of replacement was tantamount in the design for the head office of the Japanese Red Cross Society in Tokyo in 1977 as I was faced with the distasteful prospect of replacing an architectural masterpiece ravaged beyond repair. A

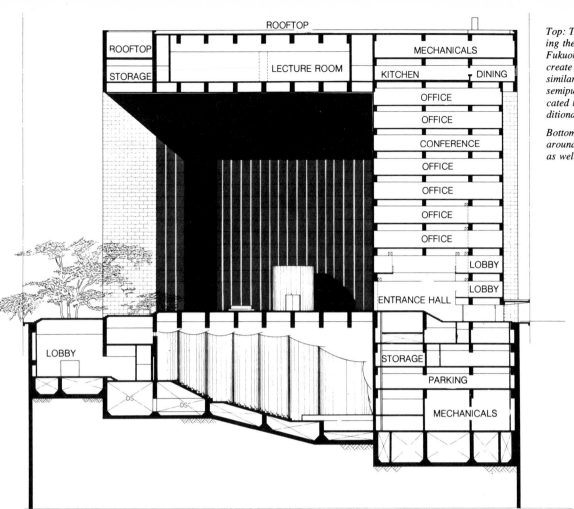

ROOFTOP

| ROOFTOP | | | | MECHANICALS | |
| STORAGE | LECTURE ROOM | | | KITCHEN | DINING |

OFFICE

OFFICE

CONFERENCE

OFFICE

OFFICE

OFFICE

OFFICE

LOBBY

LOBBY

ENTRANCE HALL

LOBBY

DS   DS

STORAGE

PARKING

MECHANICALS

Top: The urban roof sheltering the outdoor plaza of the Fukuoka Bank is intended to create an intermediary zone similar in character to the semipublic covered spaces located in private areas of traditional Japanese buildings.

Bottom: The building wraps around the en-space in plan as well as in section.

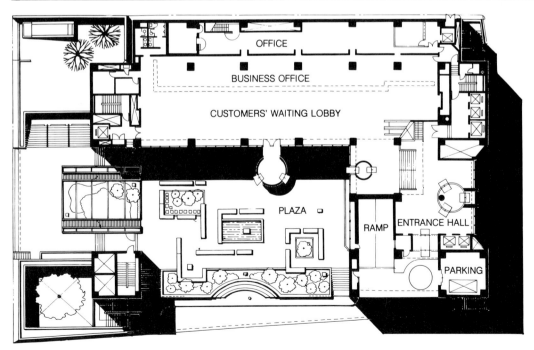

OFFICE

BUSINESS OFFICE

CUSTOMERS' WAITING LOBBY

PLAZA

RAMP   ENTRANCE HALL

PARKING

Right: A central crevice space in the Japanese Red Cross Building is an attempt to reduce the sense of oppression produced by vast wall surfaces.

Below: Part of the old structure has been incorporated into the new building; the granite window frames in the wall facing the crevice are reconstructions of the originals, which were too badly damaged to preserve.

perfect restoration and conservation of the whole building, which, of course, was my instinctive first wish in deference to the *chef d' oeuvre*, proved to be impossible due to economic considerations. As it was, we were forced to sell half the site to finance the construction of the new building. That meant that the only way Yorinaka Tsumaki's 1912 German-style building could be preserved at all would be to pick it up and move it to a new site, but nobody wanted to pay for that. The only course open to me was to capture the essence of the old headquarters and incorporate it into the new building, if indeed that is ever possible. I was also able to produce a record of the original construction and to include some of the original pieces such as windows, decor, and fixtures (or facsimilies) in the new design.

Central to this scheme is the Japanese concept of en-space bridging the gap between the two blocks. Here, I introduced the crevice, a device traditionally used in Japanese architecture to imply absence or surprise, similar perhaps to the role of the tower in medieval cities as the occasional element of surprise within a uniform urban fabric. It has the added attraction here of a purely functional rationale, as it splits the Red Cross building from the rental office space. The crack is at once the link between the twin towers, and the intermediary zone modulates the transition from outside to inside and from past to present. The jet-burner—finished Brazilian red granite facing the exterior wall is brought inside; the structural beams supporting the carport puncture the wall

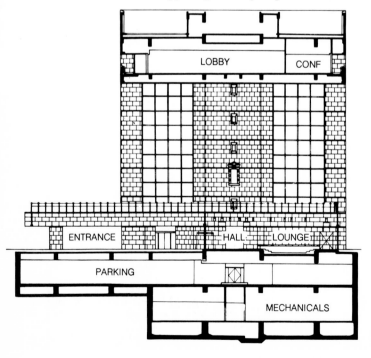

membrane; and the lobby is flooded with light, penetrating the vaulted skylight and reflecting the mood outside in the symbolic dry pond.

The pursuit of details in architectural design is a way of discovering a point of juncture, or coexistence between the structure and the materials, between technology and sensual perception. I have always been interested in the drama of the collision of two materials and have only recently begun to experiment with it. Not only do the granite-clad columns of the Red Cross facade slice directly through the mirror-glass surface (or at least appear to), but I also insert a third material or a breathing space between two clashing ones. Strips of marble restrain the carpet from hitting the wall surfaces in the special guest rooms. Traditional materials are combined with modern ones by using such techniques as inlay, bordering, and overlapping, a classic example of cultural coexistence created by the conjunction of alien elements.

I took the Buddhist notion of ambiguity and in-betweenness a stage further in my design for the Ishikawa Cultural Center in 1977. Housing an auditorium, banquet and conference facilities, and a small hotel, the building is sited adjacent to Kanazawa castle, the ancient cultural center of this part of Japan, on an abandoned baseball diamond. Again, the issue of coexistence between history and modern technology predominated the design process. The center has a low profile in deference to the scale of the surrounding area, which meant that the bulky mass of the auditorium was placed in the center of the site. Conforming to the shape of the site, the building was sliced into two fragments, splitting the auditorium from the hotel, which are restitched by the thread of lobby/entry/restaurant, leaving a cleavage of unenclosed space. To blend the building into the site, I clothed the form with traditional Rikyu gray Japanese tiles; all visible surfaces within (except the floors) are faced in aluminum. There is also a fence and a moat circumscribing the building, a redefinition of some of the older aspects of the city in modern terms.

Japanese Tradition of Mobility

The concept of time is embodied in the Japanese tradition of mobility. Our modern nomadic, fluid society has its roots in the historical shift of the capital every few years, the custom of embarking on religious pilgrimages, and the seasonal migration of agricultural workers to jobs in the cities. Movement occurs at several scales. Daily, people

commute to and from work. Seasonally, they travel between permanent and temporary residences. Annually, at least 10 percent of the Japanese move their homes. There is also a macroscale drift to major urban centers, which ought to taper off in about 25 years as people begin moving back to regional cities. As it is, over half the population lives in cities linked by a highly sophisticated transportation/communication network. All this has led to the concept of a time community, a community of individuals based on the different activities any person might perform over time, as opposed to the usual determinant of place. Time communities are populated by *homo movens*, the people of the future who will not care overly much about owning possessions and stately homes, but will instead prefer to acquire the new status symbols of free movement and extensive credit.

This suggests an architecture of movement space, which also has traditional precursors in the Japanese street. Buildings typically are open to the street, which is simultaneously a traffic artery and a living room. Historically, this sort of arrangement has been convenient for festivals, which, in the East, were mostly processionals in contrast with the mass assemblies of the West. As the mediator between public and private spaces,

the street itself could be transformed into an architecture within which day-to-day living proceeds.

The interior street is the nucleus of my scheme for the Tanzania National Headquarters Building designed for Dodoma, Tanzania, in 1972. Strung along it are the national assembly, party headquarters, and cultural center. The pedestrian spine encourages social interaction; it provides screening from the brutal African sun while permitting cross-ventilation, an organic connection between interior and exterior.

The Importance of Technology to Japan

In addition to its identification with traditional Japanese culture and religion, metabolism is inextricably bound to technology. For technology is everything to the Japanese. It is our only resource, as we have to import over 30 percent of our food and over 95 percent of our energy. The mountainous terrain accounts for four-fifths of the land, leaving precious little for human habitation. Our land is easily the most costly in the world, with plots in Tokyo averaging $10 million an acre. We

Opposite page: The exterior of the Ishikawa Cultural Center is blended into the site by cladding it with traditional Japanese tiles in a shadowy Rikyu gray tone.

Below: The roof grid of the Tanzania National Headquarters Building project is an A-frame structure which supports the assembly hall. At the vertex of the A is a large mechanical duct serving the space below and defining the interior pedestrian street.

are desperately short of housing to shelter our large, ever-increasing populace, forcing us to turn to industrialized building as a possible solution.

The Japanese very willingly imported Western technology. What they neglected to do, however, was adopt the philosophy and individualism that accompanied it. What we have achieved has been a bizarre mix of East and West. The planned obsolescence on which industry is based is a very quick, efficient, and profitable concept, unless you take into account the social and aesthetic significance of spaces and how that affects the relationship between humanity and technology. We tried to salvage what we could of this obsolescence, which was blighting the landscape with abandoned hulks of economically inefficient, but otherwise quite serviceable warehouses and factories. Taking our clues from biology, with its continual renewal and destruction of organic tissue, we conceived of a whole structure as a combination of many units with varying lifespans. It might be possible to distinguish between the fixed parts and those which would change. These could be further subdivided according to their degree of durability—how often they would need to be discarded. Then we would only have to replace the outdated parts and in this way contribute to the conservation of resources by using buildings longer, a concept that owes much to the Buddhist philosophy of cosmic change and eternal growth. We termed this "Metabolic Cycle Theory."

According to the theory, the fixed parts in buildings would be the primary structural systems. Less permanent than that would be the primary mechanical systems—the supply and return ducts, main water lines, electrical lines, and so on. Even less permanent is the main circulation system—the stairs and elevators. And the capsule is the least permanent part. It was born out of the *jiga,* the oriental *individuum* which consists of a relationship in which the individual and society, while being contradictory, include each other. Likewise the capsule is independent of the building to which it is attached. It could be defined as a device like an airplane, spaceship, or submarine which allows a person to perform complicated functions beyond his physical capabilities as a living creature so that it becomes a "home away from home." In other words, tools such as automobiles, trains, and aircraft function as dwellings and are capsulized. Or the converse could apply where the dwelling becomes a capsulized tool, as a mobile home does. The capsule, then, is the proper dwelling of *homo movens*. It is the true emancipation of the building from the land.

Systems are necessary for supporting human activities, but they are scarcely reasons for living.

They merely establish the framework within which the inhabitants of capsules can do whatever they want. In this diversified society of the future, one can paint a picture of an entirely new conception of the family as a household based on the encounter of individuals abolishing the housing unit centered on the nuclear family. The housing capsule I designed for the Theme Pavilion of Expo '70 was intended to show what such a house might look like.

The capsule is the ultimate form of prefabricated building which will make qualitative conversion of the industrial production of buildings possible. Mass produced on a selective system which goes beyond the deadly dull industrialized buildings that are the current state-of-the-art, the capsule permits an interchangeability of parts. These parts, the functional units, can easily be replaced; proliferation is possible by simply adding additional components.

Our aim is to produce space which will sensitively react to the changes in people's lifestyles. In the future, building will be defined as the state of spatial-temporal docking of more than one capsule.

In a more pragmatic vein, the actual physical design and construction of capsules suggested a systems approach due to the high level of technological sophistication required of the end product. This implied that the building is dissolved into parts and capsulized as functional units; each particular functional unit was analyzed and split into its component elements, which were then checked for usefulness and aquirability. Working backwards, the parts were recombined to see if they could be assembled in a reasonable fashion, if the scheduling sequence was feasible, if it was possible to transport and attach them into their environmental context, and, foremost, if the package would be aesthetically pleasing and no more expensive than ordinary construction.

In planning capsules, as they are mixed systems, much effort went into varying the plan types and establishing the standard and optional equipment to be included. It turned out to be quite useful to define a dynamic module. In much the same way as an automobile is made of a myriad of pipes, screws, wiring, and other gadgetry, which nobody expects to conform to a standard module, a dynamic module enables a variety of possible modules and proportioning systems to be combined. The only place where everything has to fit together is at the point of joining. This makes it possible to replace parts and to mass produce freely. Or there could be a special connector designed to make the parts mesh by relating to both elements to be connected—philosophically simi-

lar to the mediating space. To date, there are two main structural types of capsules: the link such as the Capsule House in the Theme Pavilion at Expo '70 where the functional and spatial units are clipped onto their connector; and the cubic capsule which is a package such as the Nakagin Capsule Tower completed in Tokyo in 1972.

Designed as studio apartments or hotel rooms for itinerant business executives, the Tower is the first example of a true time community in that nearly a third of the condominiums were purchased by families as an extension to their houses as playrooms or studios. Here, I borrowed traditional Tatami proportions for the dimensions of the capsules (4 by 2.5 meters, or 13 by 8 feet) and juxtaposed them with a high-technology capsule structure based on a modified shipping container, an all-welded, lightweight steel box covered with slickly painted enamel panels. But the capsules were actually built conventionally due to their tight dimensions into which many parts and wet elements had to be put. Fitting the capsules together required extremely accurate measurements with frequent inspections of the work. Erection difficulties were exacerbated by the fact that the capsules were fabricated 450 kilometers (280 miles) away from Tokyo. Since there was no storage space on the site for them, they were stored a day's drive away and trucked into Tokyo at the crack of dawn on the day they were to be attached to the tower shafts.

The building, then, is comprised of three elements: capsules, equipment, and tower shafts. Built on an artificial land base, the towers are rigid-frame structures containing circulation elements. The rack system for plumbing permits each unit to service three floors with flexible tubes making the connection between the pipes and the capsules; since sovent toilets were used, there are no vent pipes. The capsules are attached at four points to the towers with high-tension bolts so that they are in fact clipped on and plugged in.

Later, capsules were used for service and circulation elements in the Sony Tower erected in Osaka in 1975. Primarily a showcase for Sony products, this building was conceived as an information tree in harmony with Sony's image as a communications developer. The glazed escalators, elevators, and display showroom link the interior and exterior space as mediating elements.

We have been considering the capsule entirely physically. Of great importance is the philosophical background to the concept. Capsules have been conceived as weapons with which man asserts his individuality and freedom in today's chaotic world. Words like "capsule" and *"homo movens"* may be nothing more than fragments of ideas. But they are like bullets as they move the age far more powerfully and impellingly than any magnificent system of thought.

The Philosophy of Metabolism

In the past, design began in the realm of ideas, with the architect asking himself a question, for example: "What is a university?" It was considered the mission of an architect to establish an idea first and give a faithful expression to the total image. But no matter what the program, a panorama like the one obtained from the apex of a pyramid is completely meaningless if multipurpose and complex functions exist simultaneously, but without clarity. Architecture is nothing more or less than an aggregate of extremely capsulized and diverse functions; it may be defined as a group which comes into being when a number of capsules encounter each other. Accordingly, an architectural structure can be dissolved into many spaces, each with different functions. The spaces thus taken apart are capsulized, and the state where countless such capsules are conglomerated and docked in time and space can be defined as an architectural structure.

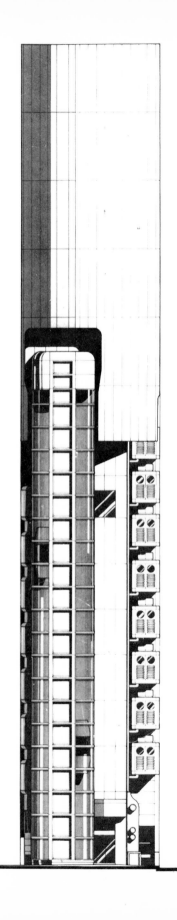

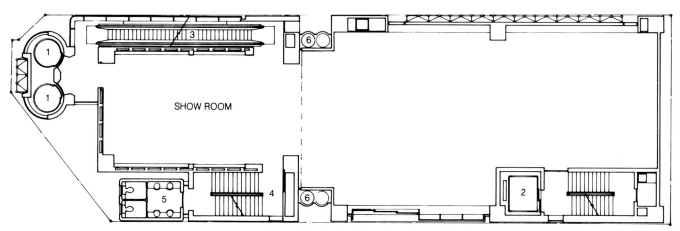

SHOW ROOM

1

1

3

6

5

4

6

2

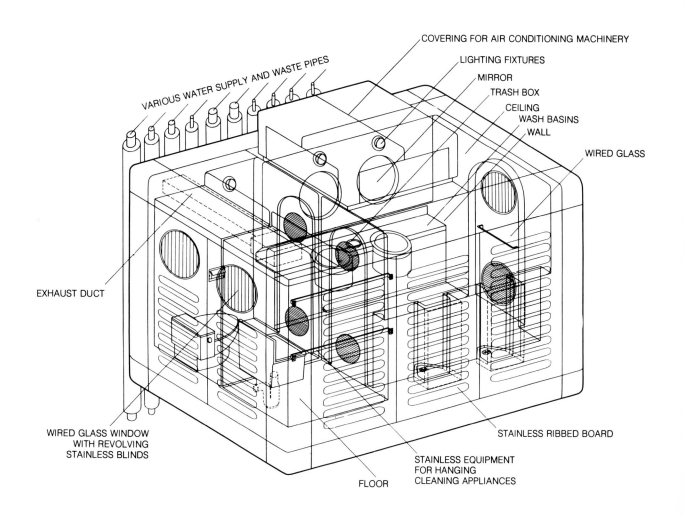

COVERING FOR AIR CONDITIONING MACHINERY

LIGHTING FIXTURES

MIRROR

TRASH BOX

CEILING

WASH BASINS

WALL

WIRED GLASS

VARIOUS WATER SUPPLY AND WASTE PIPES

EXHAUST DUCT

STAINLESS RIBBED BOARD

WIRED GLASS WINDOW
WITH REVOLVING
STAINLESS BLINDS

STAINLESS EQUIPMENT
FOR HANGING
CLEANING APPLIANCES

FLOOR

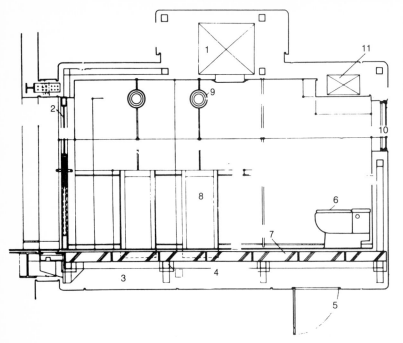

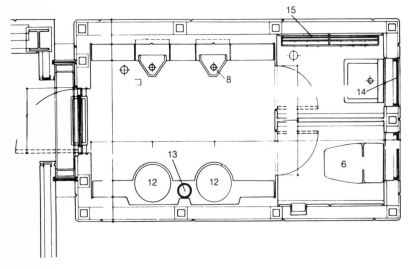

Above: Section and plan of Sony toilet capsule.
1. *Air conditioning machinery/heating pumps*
2. *Connector to main structure*
3. *Plenum for pipes*
4. *Asbestos*
5. *Access panel*
6. *Toilet*
7. *Flooring*
8. *Urinal*
9. *Lighting*
10. *Revolving window*
11. *Exhaust fan*
12. *Wash basin*
13. *Trash box*
14. *Revolving stainless steel blind*
15. *Stainless steel equipment for handing cleaning appliances*

Opposite page: Built for Expo '70 in Osaka, the Takara Beautillion synthesizes my philosophy of metabolism in that it was quickly assembled and dissembled from prefabricated components, high-technology capsules were inserted into the frame, displays were aligned along the circulation route, while the building is frayed at the edges to mediate between indoors and out.

Metabolism is best exemplified in the Takara Beautillion built for Expo '70 in Osaka. Constructed in less than a week by bolting together some 200 prefabricated steel framing units into a three-dimensional grid, the building was just as rapidly dismantled "like the falling petals of a cherry blossom tree" when its useful life as an exhibition pavilion was complete. Display panels and capsules simply slip into the interstices of the frame. There is also, of course, the possibility of adding more elements, a fact only hampered by the structural limitations inherent in an unbraced frame which are particularly consequential in earthquake-prone Japan.

The spiky frame intentionally reaches its arms out to vaguely define the outside boundary of the building. In the same way, the mediating space encompasses the plaza area with its periscopes jutting out of the ground, letting the people on the plaza glimpse the auditorium below while bringing it natural light. And people wait on the large staircase elements, a partially enclosed outside space, to penetrate within. When they finally get inside, they move along a circulation path lined with displays: an architecture of the street.

This is a high-technology building composed completely of prefabricated elements. It is a kind of architecture of the part where each element (staircase, structure, or mechanicals) is established on its own module which is best suited for its function and then interwoven. Capsules were also used for displays and for the foyer.

Metabolism, then, is a philosophy which values the preservation of relationships among architecture, society, and nature, while constantly changing with the passage of time. The basic kinetic form in which space develops is metabolism and its process is expressed as an increasing entropy. Metabolism does not presuppose any system of thought previously established and built up. It rejects all primary conceptual definition. Its effectiveness and the attention given it depend upon its relevance to the problems facing contemporary architecture and planning.

HERMAN HERTZBERGER

*Born in Amsterdam in 1932, Herman Hertzberger received his architecture degree
from the Technical University in Delft some 26 years later. That same year he opened
his own office in Amsterdam and soon began editing* Dutch Forum *together with Aldo
Van Eyck, Jacob Bakema, and others. He also started working on his first
commission, a factory addition which is constructed on top of an existing building.
This was followed by a dormitory, a building which attempts to break down the
barrier between public and private. It also includes an indoor street on the fourth level
where the married students' apartments are located. Each element such as the indoor
street lighting is programmed to play as many roles as possible, an approach which is
characteristic of his work. The block of lighting is at the same time a light fixture, a
ledge for letters and groceries, and a planter. Similar features characterize his
Montessori school where, for instance, tiny childsize strips of sandpits are garden
plots and make-believe houses, battlestations and treasure troves. More recently he
has built eight experimental houses which have been extensively and successfully
adapted or taken over by their occupants to accommodate a diversity of lifestyles, in
addition to the projects illustrated here. He is currently at work on several town
planning and urban renewal schemes.*

*His work has been exhibited and published widely. He has had articles published in
such journals as* A + U, RIBA Journal, Domus, *and* Architectural Forum. *He has
also taught extensively in America at Massachusetts Institute of Technology and
Columbia, in Canada at Toronto, and in Holland at Amsterdam and his alma mater.*

*With Centraal Beheer the
question was to make an office building that would be a
working place where everybody would feel at home: a
house for 1000 people.*

The architect has never been very human. Throughout history he has occupied himself with pyramids, temples, cathedrals, palaces, and office buildings. He has existed more to honor and celebrate the established order of the few, than to stimulate better conditions for the many: more servant of the oppressors than of the oppressed.

Whenever the architect effectively determines the environment of people on a large scale and gives it form in word and deed, he in fact contributes, as is continually being demonstrated, to the perpetuation and extension of a world where everything is too cold and too large: a grim underworld of gravestone skyscrapers, of empty squares and smooth, rejecting, untouchable walls between the asphalt that is spewed out as a choking crust over steadily enlarging areas of our towns. This whole misformed world is little more than a gigantic storage system where nobody really feels at home and everybody is an outsider. This is a no man's land from which none of us can extricate himself. It is a world of alienation.

The starting point for the design of housing is a collective interpretation by a few of the individual wishes of many, a conception formed by authorities, investors, sociologists, and architects about what people want. This conception can never be more than a stereotype to which perhaps everyone seems by and large to conform and no one person really does.

Every society is for the individual a basic given pattern to which he is subsidiary. Everyone is doomed to be the person he wants the others to see. That is the price that the individual pays to society in order to remain an insider. And so he is simultaneously possessor of and possessed by a collective pattern of behavior. Everything that is organized for people and fixed up for them will, even with the best of intentions, be experienced as imposed from above and cannot therefore be adapted and annexed by them. The boundless fear that whatever is left to itself will lead to chaos continues to gain priority, while it is in fact the conflicts and the resolving of them that are the essential function of society.

The idea of ever being able to start off with a clean slate is absurd, and moreover, disastrous when, under the pretext of its being necessary to start completely from the beginning, what already exists is destroyed so that the naked space can be filled up with impractical and sterile constructions.

Several years ago I was asked to design a new library building on the site of a well-preserved 19th-century neo-Gothic church. Rather than demolish this perfectly usable and rather unique given, we decided to design the new building as an extension of the old. My insistence on preserving the church cost us the job. When we do away with what has gone before us, pay no attention to what we still possess, and thus make no use of the accumulation of images at our disposal, we nip the possibility of renewal in the bud.

We could assume, as many do, that all of what architects do is unnecessary, since people left to themselves could provide for their own needs better than we can if only we give them the room. One need only consider the conditions under which people live (or subsist) all over the world; everywhere it has been the people themselves who, without even a minimum of outside help, have gone on making of the given conditions what could be made of them. But would this not be to abuse the inventions and apparently limitless adaptability with which people, however confined their circumstances, make do with the impossible, making the unusable useful and the uninhabitable habitable?

Changing the world is a step-by-step process. A revolution is nothing more than the sum total of infinitely many small pieces which must be fitted together, one by one like a gigantic jigsaw puzzle. Any of these steps can only occur as a change of attitude, a self-generating process enveloping the whole of society. Like everybody else, architects can contribute and maybe add a few pieces which fit into the great puzzle. Architects must not just

show what is possible; they must show what should be possible for everyone. Everything that we make has to offer a helping hand to the people to let them become more intimate with their surroundings, with each other, and with themselves. It has to do with making shoes that fit instead of pinch.

The more somebody is personally able to influence his surroundings, the more involved and attentive he becomes, and also the more likely he will be to give them his love and care. However devotedly we may carry out our work, we can never match objects with people as exactly as when they do it by themselves and for each other by way of the love and care which can arise between them.

The task of the architect is to free in the users themselves whatever they think they need by evoking images in them which can lead to their own personally valid solutions.

Form: The Vehicle of Changing Meanings

What matters with forms, just as with words and sentences, is how they are read, what images they evoke in the readers. Seen through a different eye and in different situations, a form will evoke other associations and thus inspire other images that can acquire new meanings. It is this experiential phenomenon that provides the key to a new notion of form which we can use to make things more adjustable to various situations. In its capacity to acquire a meaning and surrender it again, without substantially changing itself, form becomes a potential vehicle of changing meanings, innately receptive to being colored in, for, and by various situations, always capable of stimulating new images.

When we see a bit of pottery in the form of a plate, it refers us to a table setting, meals, china cupboards, or perhaps watering the plants or mix-

We proposed to convert the neo-Gothic church in Gronigen, Holland, into a university library by weaving the older structure into the newer one.

ing watercolors, depending on our aims and intentions. The fragmented plates which Gaudi has used to tile the curved terrace walls in the Parc Guell in Barcelona break through the accepted pottery images and become building material. A plate in fragments is no longer a unit on its own. Each distinct fragment, like its neighbors, becomes an accessory to the wall as a building stone. The old image is strong enough to survive even when broken. But it mingles with the other image, that of the wall, permitting the form to be read in different ways. The result is both ambiguity and plurality in the elementary sense, the beginning of another understanding of form. These plates are the once and for all expression of an artist's imagination. The process is irreversible; we can never again eat from them, we cannot sell them to an antiques dealer, and there is no need to anyway.

Forms with a too strongly defined purpose are too strongly committed. What is expected of the user and what is or is not permitted has already been too clearly worked out, leaving the user subsidiary to the form and to the implicit assignment it suggests.

Designing ought to mean a better disciplining of the material with an eye to getting more in return for your money. Everything that is given a deliberate form should be appropriate for the job that's expected of it by different people, in different situations, at different moments, and in endless retake.

One might assume that we only have to make unemphatic empty cartridges, as neutral as possible, so as to allow the occupants optimal freedom to fulfill their specific wants. However paradoxical it may seem, it is highly questionable whether such a degree of freedom might not have a paralyzing effect. It is like the sort of menu that offers such an endless array of dishes that, instead of making you hungry, dulls your appetite. When too many possibilities are offered, the choice you would make gets lost in the melee of all the other

Instead of the usual big sandpit in this Montessori School, the walls have been used to divide up the space into a large number of very small rooms in which the children can play.

possible choices; we could then speak of "freedom noise."

Unlimited freedom may hold great potential, but there is no spark to start the motor. The central point here is that people, in their dependence on themselves and on each other, and the fundamental limitation that this means, cannot free themselves from the systems of significations and the underlying systems of values and valuation by which they are confined without being given a helping hand. Everyone needs an incitement, a helping hand, to motivate and stimulate him to fit his environment to himself and make it his own. These instigators must be so designed that they summon up images in everyone which, through being significantly projected, lead to associations which stimulate an individual use, that is, precisely the use he had need of in his particular situation. The more associations something evokes, the more people and the more of their personal situations will be able to resonate with it.

The Architect's Musée Imaginaire of Forms

The main difficulty in architecture is that in order to present raw material containing intentions which will accommodate the users, you have to know as the architect what will or will not be evocative for them. For each thing you want to make, you have to summon up by yourself all images of all the users and integrate these as intentions in what you present. And what other way is there to achieve this than by putting yourself in the other's place. What holds for everyone in general holds for the architect also in the professional sense, namely, he must look well and listen well. For the tools which matter to him are not his ruler and set of compasses, but above all his eyes and ears.

When we are designing, we have to explore our memory continuously for all the experiences that can be brought to bear on what we are making. What we create can be different from, but never more than, what has become part of ourselves as experience. By referring each one back to its fundamentally unchangeable ingredients, we then try to discover what our images have in common and find thus the cross section of the collection, the unchangeable, underlying element of all the examples which in its plurality can be the form-generating point.

Many people believe that the dilemma implicit in the subjectivity of our imaginative faculty can be resolved by shifting the emphasis to scientific research, that this is the source of more objective information on human needs. But since such research methodologically starts from a hypothesis, the audacity—or lack of it—of the hypothesis will dictate the limits of the result. We cannot get around the difficulty or escape our dependence on subjective experience in this way.

The only available escape from the fundamental limitations of our imaginative faculty lies in directing our attention more to the experiences we all have in common, the collective memory, some of it innate, some of it transmitted and acquired, which in one way or another must be at the base of our common experiential world. It can be likened to the relationship between language and speech. We each use language in our own way; as long as we keep more or less within the framework of recognized declensions and rules and use recognizable words, the message comes across. Indeed we can assume an underlying objective structure of forms which we will call "arch-forms," a derivative of which is what we get to see in a given situation. The whole *musée imaginaire* of forms can then be conceived of as an infinite variety out of which people help themselves, in constantly changing variation, to forms which in the end refer back to the fundamentally unchangeable and underlying reservoir of arch-forms.

Making something new each time would not only be useless, but impossible anyway. What is possible is to present the same in such a way that something else can be read into it.

A Question of Finding the Right Size

The world which is regulated by a person himself, and not for him, will be smaller. It will be built from small dimensions of workable units no larger than a person or group needs and can devotedly care for on his or their own. Each unit will be more intensively used and therefore shown to the best advantage. Articulation thus leads to "increased capacity," which means a greater return on the available material, or getting by with less material by using it more intensively. Everything has to have its right size, and this is the measure necessary to its being employed as completely as possible. And if we are to make things no bigger than necessary and no bigger than is handy and usable, this will amount to having to make almost everything much smaller.

It is a question of the right dimensions, placing, beat, interval—the right articulation—that things and people offer each other. Irregularities such as differences in level and unevenness of the building line occur frequently. Instead of trying hard to iron them out, we should direct ourselves to forming them consciously in such a way that they can be exploited. Walls, posts, bars, and gutters are also devices of articulation and can all form an increased capacity for adhesion. They can be used as primitive elements of what we could call the basic grammar of the architect. In their diverse outward forms they are constant incentives for use in daily life.

However far the designer goes, it is the occupants who go on to put the finishing touches to a building once they have taken it over, constantly changing and renewing it and constantly taking more complete possession of it. They interpret the building in their own way. The more diverse the ways in which the building allows for completion, the more people there will be who can feel at home in it. For the office building of Centraal Beheer the question was to make a working place where everybody would feel at home—in fact, a house for 1,000 people.

Centraal Beheer

Centraal Beheer is a cooperative insurance company headquarters designed in 1973. The bulk of its activity is the routine clerical work necessary for processing claims, receiving payments, and so on. Formerly housed in ordinary speculative offices in Amsterdam, it was plagued by high rents and a high staff turnover which were alleviated by the move to the new building with its high proportion of social amenities in Apeldoorn.

The building can be divided geographically into four quadrants, three of which contain the office spaces, with a "wingspread" of central area in between. The working spaces are large rooms, continuous yet articulated in such a way that a group or individual can appropriate a com-

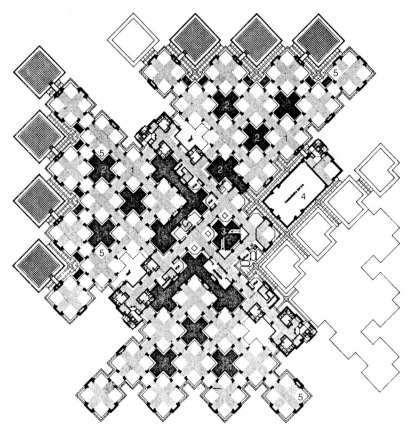

Above: Typical floor plan of Centraal Beheer.
1. Circulation
2. Voids
3. Central wingspread
4. Mechanical services
5. Typical workstations

Opposite page, left: Four possible office furniture arrangements.

Opposite page, right: The essential incompleteness of the building, the grayness, and the bare concrete are colored in by the inhabitants.

prehensive place for himself. The open relationship with floors below as well as above gives a certain feeling of belonging. The voids are breathing space, the built-in margin that prevents overcrowding. The basic 3 by 3 meter (10 by 10 feet) space forming the corner of each main element, or "island," can accommodate from one to four workstations. It is defined by a pair of substantial T-columns, by a low block wall on the edge of a void, and by deep downturned beams lining the "corridor" walls (and enclosing the mechanical ducts). The offices are both higher and brighter than the adjacent circulation areas, serving to further heighten the sense of place. This arrangement forms the frame of reference and starting point for the initiative of the users; precisely because the organization of the whole has been done for them, the users can devote themselves entirely to the things which especially matter to them. As far as the individual workstation is concerned, the simple facts of choosing one's own lighting and desk type and having the possibility to dress it up however one likes in an ad-hoc fashion with flowers, plants, posters, and what-have-you allow one to take possession of the space. It is the fundamental unfinishedness of the building, the grayness, the naked concrete, and the many other imposed (but also concealed) free-choice possibilities that are meant to stimulate the occupants to add their own color, so that everyone's choice and therefore his standpoint is brought to the surface. This building is an example of my thesis that what architects should be making is "the wall" on which everyone can write down, in his own way, whatever he wants to communicate to others. The information which remains under discussion will be legible for a long time; that which is no longer germaine will be submerged by other accounts, the distinctive marks of other and altered inhabitants. This is tangibility in its most literal sense, and it is the antithesis of the neat, orderly, alienated world from which we want to wrest ourselves.

We have deliberately not indicated a boundary between offices. For if the design started from the idea of division of the whole into private premises, no doubt everyone would have done his best to make something of it for himself. A strict, built-in division between what is private and what is public would have been established a priori. But now an in-between area has been created, the intermingling zone of the strictly private areas, the workstations, and the public domain, the "street." Specifically, the building has been designed as a structure with a basic inalterable structural zone that manifests itself throughout the building; it includes the main mechanical ducts

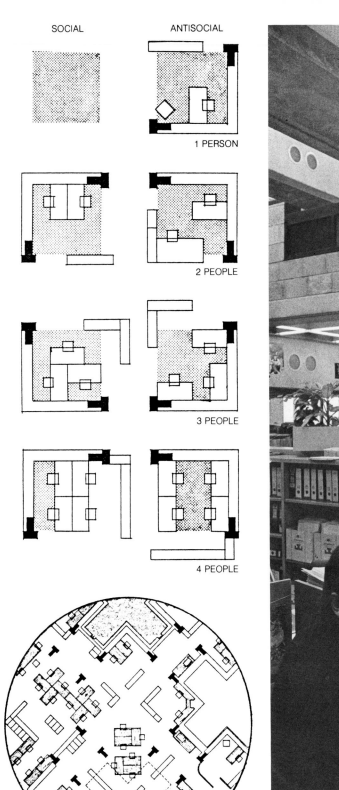

SOCIAL   ANTISOCIAL

1 PERSON

2 PEOPLE

3 PEOPLE

4 PEOPLE

Like a little village, there are many cafes or coffeebars in Centraal Beheer where one can go to sit, talk, and watch other people whenever one wants.

The system of numerous heavy columns defines small space units in such a way as to promote their articulation. In spite of what one might expect, this enlarges rather than diminishes the option of adjustment by the inhabitants.

and coincides with the main circulation pattern as expected. There is also a secondary structure of small concrete block partitions that are interpretable and variable: forms are only designed to a coarse grain, leaving allocation of workstations and furnishing arrangements to the discretion of the users, so the space can be constantly changed. Wherever resolving conflicts might lead to people reaching more agreement with each other, we ought to build them in rather than try to avoid them.

In a larger sense this happens with the public streets that cross the center of the building. Centraal Beheer is accessible at many points; no particular entrance claims to be the main entrance, or rather, all entrances are main entrances. This openness is intended to contribute to the reconciliation of building and street, of public and private. Mother and children may have a walk in the building to see where father is working and what he is doing. They may have a drink together in one of the coffeebars in the central area. Coffee in fact is no longer brought into the working spaces at fixed hours; instead one goes to a coffeebar whenever and as often as one wishes. The family may even lunch together in the restaurant, as many do. Here an attempt has been made to produce an environment which will allow a great variety of social contacts. Contrary to the normal canteen with its repetition of uniform tables for six or eight people for a uniform social stencil plate, there is room for a varied and consequently richer social pattern.

This building is a hypothesis. Whether it can withstand the consequences of what it brings into being depends on the way in which it conforms to the behavior of its occupants with the passing of time.

Below: Plan of the De Drie Hoven village green.

Key:
 1. Shop
 2. Storeroom for chairs
 3. Storeroom for instruments
 4. Podium
 5. Laundry
 6. Public terrace
 7. Billiard hall
 8. Smoking corner
 9. Occupational therapy
 10. Bar
 11. Buffet
 12. Library
 13. Social work
 14. Hairdresser
 15. Gyro branches
 16. Post office
 17. Bank

Opposite page, top: Houses should allow the occupiers to convert them to their own needs not only inside, but also outside. This woman has made a front porch in the corridor in front of her apartment at De Drie Hoven.

Opposite page, bottom: One of the most popular seating areas is around the billiard room.

De Drie Hoven

The other, rather extensive building, designed in the same period although constructed later, is the residential complex De Drie Hoven intended for physically or mentally handicapped people, most of whom have reached an advanced age. All of them need care and especially attention. Like Centraal Beheer, this building is an attempt to invite the inhabitants into as active a role as possible in their environment and consequently offer a helping hand to establishing relationships with the other inhabitants. Everything possible has been done to avoid a hospital atmosphere, which tends to imply an emphasis on treatment. Just because the nursing and sanitary facilities control the "patient's" life to such a large extent, they must not

be allowed to dominate the living quarters, while always being available.

This building is also essentially unfinished, enabling the occupants to alter it in accord with their changing needs. This in fact was a questionable experiment since the inhabitants on the whole are in such bad condition that one might not expect them to exhibit a great deal of concern. Still, the common opinion is that everything is supposed to be done for them instead of by them, and their environment as it is usually made adds to their passiveness rather than stimulating them to use any degree of vitality they still possess. The residents' limited mental and physical capacities make it impossible for them to go out into the town, so as much as possible of what the town has to offer has been brought to them. The intent was to create an environment in which each person,

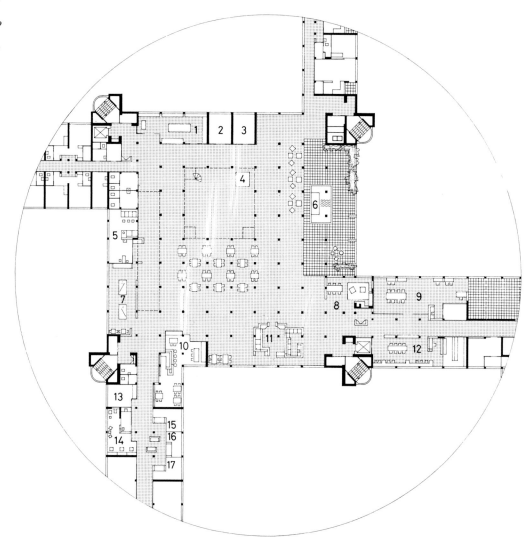

Right: This man has made his own garden on a terrace at De Drie Hoven.

Below, left: Plan and section of his terrace garden.

Below right: One of the many roof terraces at De Drie Hoven.

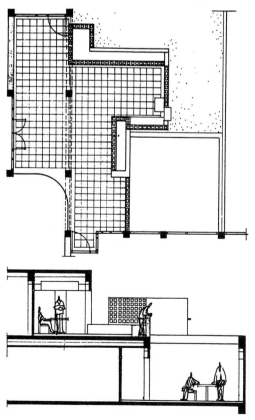

according to his limitations, would have the greatest choice of communication on the basis of a varied social pattern within the singular world of a small town forced into an isolation greater than desirable.

The requirements for the different sections of the buildings are incorporated into a common building order: a system of columns, beams, and floors whereby, in a fixed and consistently applied module, a large amount of freedom in the utilization of space arose within the limits set by the system. From the very beginning the plan was programmed to enable it to fulfill the large variety of requirements and regulations which had to be met, and blocks of different dimensions can be added to it as desired. In this way a structure was created which was then filled in according to the needs of that moment. The structural language is assumed to be great enough to enable it to incorporate subsequent additions, however chaotic, without its unity being disturbed. So a structure comes into being in which many things can be altered while it is in use and where the occupants, improvising if need be, can find answers to needs which could not be anticipated during its construction.

All the living units are situated along passageways which may be regarded as streets. They also have their own front doors, porches, and where possible, windows with a view over the street. The front doors are made so that the top half can be opened separately from the bottom. This enables those who are feeling lonely to open their homes informally to others and makes relationships between neighbors easier.

Where finish, lighting, and space are concerned, the indoor streets have been designed so that there are many places offering the chance to make contacts even on a short walk. On the many different floors adjoining the indoor streets are many small roof terraces. These are adjacent to the communal living rooms which each serve eighteen units. One could say that the communal living rooms lend themselves to neighborly contacts. The squares near the central staircase allude to the districts of the town, inducing contacts of a less binding nature. The central meeting space, nicknamed "the village green," is comparable to a town center, a sort of communal living room suitable for a variety of uses ranging from fashion shows to concerts to religious services. There is also provision for those who wish to indulge in the cosier activities of drinking coffee and playing cards.

In addition the complex also boasts such amenities as shops, laundry, bar, library, billiard hall, hairdresser, bank, giro branch, and hobby room. Every remote corner is entirely accessible inside and by elevator.

While the land surrounding the buildings is officially owned by the complex, it is permanently open to everyone. Much of it is divided into small victory gardens for the use of both the residents and the neighborhood people. Eventually the greenhouse facilities could be instrumental in setting up a system enabling the residents themselves to supply the complex with plants and flowers. And the building proper becomes a public area through its many entries. If the administration decides that De Drie Hoven has something to offer outsiders as well, a more intensive, mutually beneficial interchange could occur. For example, elderly and disabled people from the area might like to use the facilities available here: cafe, restaurant, laundry, and sun terrace, while others might be willing to work, perhaps on a part-time basis, in the building. It is then essentially unfinished, much as a town center is constantly being revised within its basic street system according to changing requirements.

Musiek Centrum Vredenburg

Both Centraal Beheer and De Drie Hoven are, each in a different way, permanently occupied by people whose intense relationship with their building makes them inhabitants. The Musiek Centrum Vredenburg in Utrecht is more of a visitors' building, in the sense that, except for the relatively small number of staff members, there are no permanent occupants to be expected whatsoever and consequently no attempts to invest any personal love and care. If the central area of Centraal Beheer and the pattern of interior streets and the village green in De Drie Hoven were to be considered as public, Musiek Centrum Vredenburg is a public realm all over. It is made of a conglomerate and variety of qualities that may accommodate a rich pattern of relationships.

It also picks up the notion of the building as a microcosm of the town. Here the shops, offices, lounges, and cafes in the internal streets are at once part of the building and part of the street pattern of the town. But mostly this project is an effort to demystify the ritual elements of a concert and replace them by another kind of celebration. With the advent of the long-playing record, the motives of concert-goers have changed. This auditorium is designed for the audience to see and surround the musical performance as well as to hear it. With a concert it is not the most perfect

Top: The facade fabric of Utrecht's Musiek Centrum Vredenburg is woven from many human size parts; the same few elements are used throughout, yet each is recombined differently. Balconies and roof terraces can be reached from the galleries inside.

Above: An interior street is a microcosm of the town with its street signs and shop windows.

Right: Musiek Centrum Vredenburg is highly articulated in an effort to capture the fine grain of the town. Wrapped around the concert hall are shops, restaurants, and an exhibition area.

balance of sound that counts; people rather like to be aware of just those irregularities of an orchestral performance that the multitrack sound mixing of the recording studio tries so hard to eliminate. This auditorium has to be used for all sorts of performances. The architect must involve himself in the organizing of the events that will stretch the building to the limits of its flexible potential.

The building, rather than being an apparatus, becomes an instrument that should be played. The instrument has capacities which the performer knows how to extract, and the way in which this happens defines the freedom which it can generate for each of its performers.

The pretension inherent in making buildings which have distinct form, distinct spatial effect, distinctly different lighting, and different building materials must justify itself by improving the situation of the people who inhabit them, or rather by offering them a helping hand to improve their conditions by themselves. A new building is the prepared ground on which the people who will inhabit it can reappraise relationships, involvements, and responsibilities. The architect will then have a lot more to do than translate a given program into form. He is in a position to demonstrate that the personal interest of all those involved can be realized by organizing space. Through his proposals he can further animate people into thinking up other new possibilities. Such a reappraisal leads unavoidably to changes which have to be undergone and absorbed by those involved.

Form makes itself, and that is less a question of invention than of listening well to what a person and thing want to be.

Unlike many concert halls, Musiek Centrum Vredenburg is arranged so that the audience surrounds the performers. While the acoustics may not be perfect, performances are much more intimate than in a more traditional hall.

JOHN JOHANSON

In 1939 John Johansen received a Bachelor of Science from Harvard. In 1942 he acquired a Bachelor of Architecture and soon after a Master of Architecture from the Harvard Graduate School of Design. In the post-war years, he established his own practice. His early works were rather orthodox modern, which he has called ''Renaissance by comparison with his later buildings.'' Gradually his buildings moved from very heavy monolithic concrete to a separateness of forms expressing distinct functional and structural parts and motivated by a greater concern for how buildings work to accommodate the needs of their occupants. The transition from what he calls his first ''modern building,'' Clark University's Goddard Library, to his own recently constructed house is startling. The former has been described as the ''rear end of the Xerox machine'' and was influenced by the organization of electronic circuitry, but still shows the lingering influences of Brutalism and Le Corbusier's la Tourette. Functionally, served spaces are distinguished from service spaces and circulation lines, a direct influence of Louis Kahn's work in the 1950s. The latter building, his own house, in contrast, is lightweight, flexible, improvised from industrialized catalog parts of steel and plastic, with rooms and platforms suspended or outrigged from a steel frame, with the possibility of permutation and change. This development has led to his current interest, an architecture of kinetics.

Johansen has received two honorary Doctor of Fine Arts degrees, has been president of the Architectural League of New York, and is a member of the American Institute of Arts and Letters. He was the recipient of the Medal of Honor from the New York Chapter of the American Institute of Architects and the Honor Award from the national American Institute of Architects. He also was architect in residence at the American Academy in Rome. Johansen has been a professor at Columbia, Yale, and Pratt Institute and a visiting critic and lecturer throughout the United States and abroad. His buildings have been extensively published and exhibited at the Museum of Modern Art in New York and in Moscow, Berlin, and Tokyo, while his articles have been published in the American Scholar *as well as journals of the architectural profession.*

The Oklahoma Theater Center is comprised of three theater components plugged into a base. The components have been simply assembled out of available hardware–light steel framing and cladding, plain wood decking, and industrial tubing throughout–and joined in an ad hoc fashion.

Unlike the theoretician, analyst, critic, or academic, the practicing architect must draw upon the experience of his own design practice, upon what he can record of his pragmatic search for what he perceives architecture to be. In this search some of us are concerned with what we have done and are doing and where our search will lead us. Most of us think we know our direction and have some clue to our further achievements in the context of a mainstream in current architectural history. Yet often enough, we don't, and it takes some more analytic mind or some other critic to either "put us in our place" or put us in some place, relative to other professional works.

Many architects are intuitive rather than rational; they don't deal entirely in established or proven fact, but from some "sense" of how things are or might be. Although increasingly our profession draws on people with special knowledge, it still deals not with just the scientific, actual, literal truth, but with poetic truth, with concepts, ideas, expressiveness. As a practicing architect, then, I can only offer some observations of myself, my search for what I believe architecture might be, and a sequence of statements and structures which may illustrate this.

After a rather nonlinear search in my early career, I have more recently come to see buildings and building complexes in terms of their parts: that is, individuation. Admittedly this is an analytic approach, yet only through analysis have I been able to deal with synthesizing the final programs and their accommodation in terms of construction. Starting first with an analysis of a program, I begin to translate it into architectural terms by drawing up an inventory of elements to scale and laying them out like an exploded assembly drawing of a machine. At this point there is no attempt to make it look like a machine, but merely to borrow the principles of its organization.

Place It, Support It, Connect It: Typing the Parts

For some time, I have considered that there are three essential elements in architecture: (1) enclosures, generalized or specific, to accommodate function, which are static and contained; (2) elements which serve as access, or circulation, in the

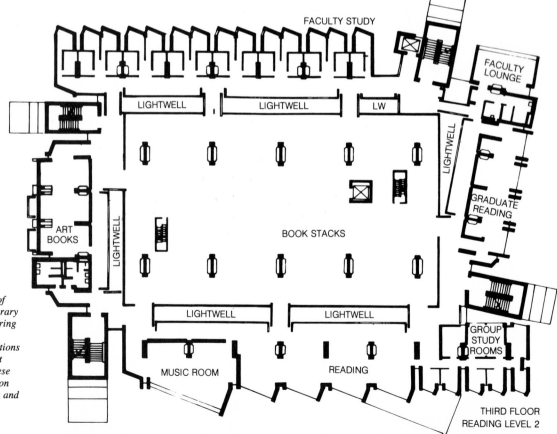

Around the central box of books in the Goddard Library of Clark University is a ring of specialties and interchangeable reading functions supported by five distinct structural frames. To these were added the circulation elements for both people and mechanical services.

FACULTY STUDY

FACULTY LOUNGE

LIGHTWELL   LIGHTWELL   LW

LIGHTWELL

GRADUATE READING

ART BOOKS

LIGHTWELL

BOOK STACKS

LIGHTWELL   LIGHTWELL

GROUP STUDY ROOMS

MUSIC ROOM   READING

THIRD FLOOR
READING LEVEL 2

kinetic function of moving people and mechanical services; and (3) structural elements which hold it all up in some sort of mutually agreeable disposition. In concept and procedure I see it as simple as (1) "place it" (the enclosures); (2) "connect it" (provide access); (3) "support it" (hold it together structurally). However, the sequence might be in reverse: starting with a structural frame to which are attached enclosures later to be connected. Or starting with a circulation system, add structure and then enclosures. Thinking in terms of these three elements has freed me from lingering Beaux Arts attitudes still prevalent in what we mistakenly accept as our modern buildings.

The first building where I applied this principle was the Goddard Library at Clark University. Completed in 1968, the library has literally five separate structural frames, each supporting a range of functional enclosures that form the specialized reading spaces. These enclosures were interchangeable, and although not actually "plug in-pull out," they were rigged and rerigged in the process of design to achieve the best interrelationship of functional parts. Architectural vitality, or the sense of life in a building, was important to me here, yet architectural composition was given little concern. To the elements of structure and enclosure were added the people-moving devices: bridges joining the inner and outer buildings, exterior fire stairs and elevator, plus the mechanical distribution system expressed vividly throughout the building. This building of concrete and brick is perhaps a bit heavy, but it was a start for me.

The profusion of small reading rooms and carrels attached to the main structure of the Goddard Library is an attempt to borrow from electronics.

Electronic Circuitry: Grouping the Parts

In a further effort to free myself from myself—from habits of thinking—and from the profession with its institutional resistance to change, I seized upon electronics as a more sophisticated technical field to borrow from, since in fact it is the electronic age we now live in. For the *American Scholar* in 1966, I wrote an article entitled "An Architecture for the Electronic Age." Prompted by the observations of Marshall McLuhan, I suggested six possible ways in which, through the retraining of our perceptive habits, our architecture would be changed and accepted by a new client whose perceptive habits, due to the same exposure, would also have to be retrained. Of particular concern to me was not so much the actual imitation of electronic devices appearing in our buildings, so-called techno-aesthetics, nor the bombardment of TV images which has prompted the explosion of woodsy, funk, shed roofs, and supergraphics, but rather the organization upon which electronic devices are actually constructed. I wanted to borrow the underlying ordering principles and their systematic logic and use them as a model for architectural methodology.

We have a great deal to learn from electronics, but even the simplest circuit will illustrate a basic organization of three principal elements, which suggest their architectural counterparts. First, there is the "chasis," representing the structural frame; second, there are "components," with subcomponents attached to them which further define the function of that component, representing in architecture, functional enclosures; and third, there is the circuiting system, the "harnesses," which represent channels for the circulation of people and mechanical services. By identifying and assembling a given program of building requirements on the strength of this ordering device, I had freed myself from that Beaux Arts design principle which still lingers in the work of most contemporary architects: that is, "the tasteful arrangement of compositional elements." In such an organization, components representing various functions can be changed. Subcomponents representing various subfunctions, supportive functions, "servant spaces," as Louis Kahn said in the 1950s, can be added or discarded, thereby qualifying more explicitly the nature of that accommodation for a particular function or human event. Also, circuiting, or the circulation routes, can be rerigged to make for different interaction; other circuiting systems can be overlayed to operate independently as long as there is no "short circuiting."

In the design of the Oklahoma Theater Center in Oklahoma City (begun in 1966 and completed in 1970), the three theaters comprise major com-

Based on the ordering principles of circuitry, a building can be split into the structural chasis, the functional components, and the circulation and servicing harnesses.

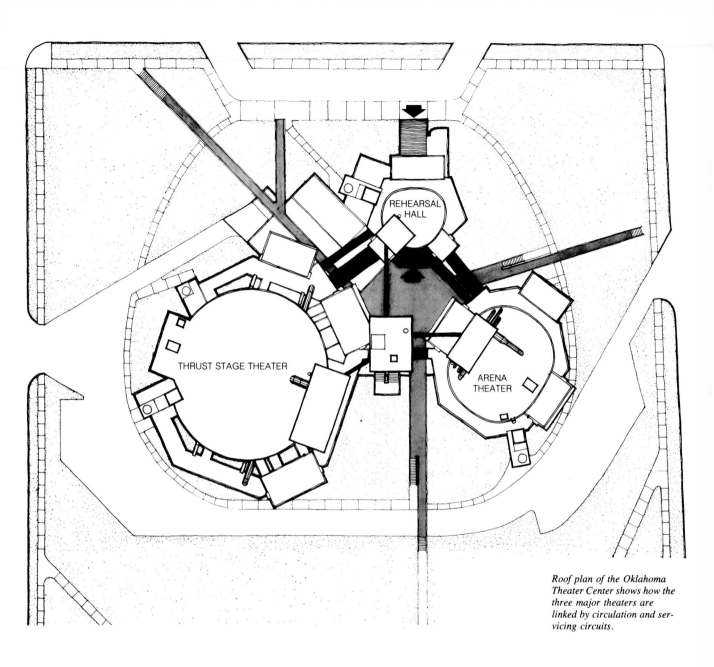

REHEARSAL
HALL

THRUST STAGE THEATER

ARENA
THEATER

*Roof plan of the Oklahoma
Theater Center shows how the
three major theaters are
linked by circulation and servicing circuits.*

place it—

support it—

connect it—

I began the design of the Oklahoma Theater Center by locating the major functional components where they would be most appropriate. Then the structures were selected from catalogs (like the rest of the building materials). Finally, the components were connected by their ducts and circulation tubes.

ponents with subcomponents—lounges, offices, toilets—attached to them. The three components are plugged into a base or chasis. The circuiting is intricate and made up of five subcircuits: (1) a corridor layout in the base connecting all understage areas; (2) a confluence of paths by means of bridges connecting the sidewalks over the roof of the base to the public gardens; (3) the automobile circuit passing under these three bridges, connecting entrances, parking, and service; (4) the theater-goers tube system which leads from ticket office and lobby to the three theaters and to "seating trays"; (5) the overhead distribution of chilled water from the cooling tower to the three air conditioning units above each theater. Each component, its structure, and circuit perform in a way as a group, or "subset," with utter disregard, in a formalist sense, for the other. The subset is recognized as a working unit—"pattern recognition," to use an IBM term. What might have been architectural chaos is held together and governed by the strength of the ordering device. The aesthetic impact results from a rich spatial effect of freely assembled parts; parts which with some variation still clearly represent their category and explain what their performance is.

Ad Hochism: Assembling the Parts

Another building of my design is the Columbus Elementary School (begun in 1967 and completed in 1969). In this organization prefabricated classrooms are assembled into three student age groups, connected by sloping tubes and articulated by glassed-in landings, or nodes. Each classroom group is also accessible by means of ramps at the periphery, carrying out the original intention of a "walk-to school." It must be said that this school and the Oklahoma Theater are intentionally ad hoc in execution. At a time when I was weary of pretentiousness, perfection, and eloquence in my work and that of other architects, I turned to improvisation, economy of means, direct solutions, even humor. "Ad hocism" may be said to describe this attitude and approach. It deals with immediacy, the here and now, with what most effective course of action can be taken without deliberation. In construction, the architect might design a building from locally available materials or of industrial predesigned and prefabricated products, even standard colors, selected from catalogs. Now what motivates the architect in this odd pursuit? First, there is the very practical advantage of producing a building more quickly, efficiently, and economically, particularly in remote or marginal site conditions. However, out of these very conditions and methods there develop challenges and demands for ingenuity, improvisations, which become exhilerating not only to the architect but to the viewer of the completed work. Out of adversity, ingenuity, directness, and immediacy develops an aesthetic value. In these two buildings, much care was given to the exact articulation of the connections. However most of the joinery was determined on site, in what might be called "in-situ detailing." God was not in my details, and I didn't at that time particularly want him, or her, there.

To me, there has never been any doubt as to the greater importance of the message compared with the grammar used in conveying it. What these buildings lack in refinement and eloquence, they gain in direct, forceful expression of their performance. As there is slang in the literate world, defined as effective, brash, colorful, sometimes crude or impudent, so there is slang in the visual language of architecture. It is through acceptance of a new, more forceful speech that language, particularly the "American language," is continually updated and enriched. The same is indeed true for the language of architecture.

Permutation: Reshuffling the Parts

Increasingly, programs are being written with flexibility, adjustment, and growth possibilities. The unadmitted fact is that we cannot write a program for just the present without the building becoming functionally obsolete within a short time, which is also a poor financial investment. If we assume that the nature of our accommodation will change in the near future, then we must write programs not for the present, but for the future as well. Obviously buildings which follow such a program must also be capable of changing. This appears to be the familiar concept of "open-ended planning," in which we do not attempt to solve all problems or make all decisions now, but solve for various possible future requirements. Rare is the programmer or architect in a time of rapid social and technological change who can truly assume that he can deal with the present alone; a developer or financier who risks the sure possibility of functional obsolescence is surely short-sighted.

The next step in my search was toward "permutation," defined as the possible interchange of parts within a particular system. Permutation implies systems. As the theory of architectural de-

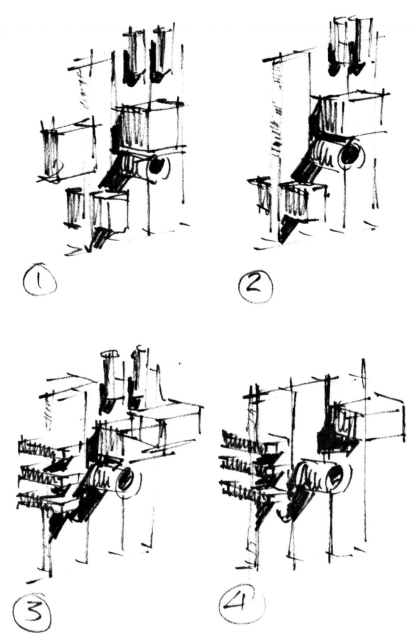

A building reshuffling its parts was the next step in my search for an architecture.

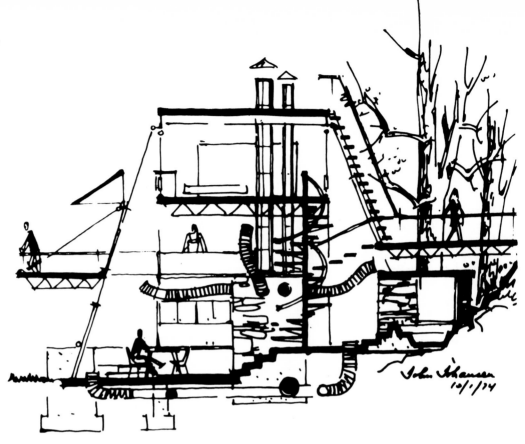

My own house was designed to be an unsophisticated, permutable, inexpensive, and easily constructed building system.

sign within systems—closed systems, open systems, mixed systems, and the "techno-aesthetics" of Archigram 1964—had already appeared, I turned to some of their proposals. In the 12 years since they introduced the principle of plug-in and clip-on, there has been no application of this in an actual or literal sense, with the exception of one or two works by Japanese architects. There is always the usual time lapse between design concept and its acceptance as part of the architectural idiom, just as there is between a concept in pure science and marketable products developed through applied science. In the case of plug-in, the building technique is easily within our reach and the aesthetic image has already been expressed, but most important are the advantages this concept offers in terms of greater functional accommodation and more profitable long-term financing.

Because of this, the design of my own house in 1972 was to be a very natural, timely development in my continuing concern for the part. The design of this house was based upon two requirements: (1) that it be a system, not particularly sophisticated, yet involving permutation; and (2) that I could build it pretty much with my own hands. It was therefore to be simply conceived, inexpen-

sive, and made of easily available materials. A steel frame, three stories high with square base and tapered sides, was devised with 64 attachment points, 32 on the interior and 32 brought through the plastic skin to the exterior. From these points platforms and rooms could be hung. The platforms could be erected in a few hours; rooms would take longer. To brace this basic steel frame, diagonal cross cables were placed to prevent wracking, as the weight might shift if platforms and rooms were to be moved about. One room is presently hung by two cables from the roof framing on the interior. Decks are suspended out from two sides, while one platform extends as a bridge from a second level to a rock ledge some 30 feet (9 meters) away. Future developments are probably a deck on the fourth side with stair to grade and possibly a midlevel platform in the living room. Instead of thwarting remodeling and change, the system encourages it. Life in this house becomes a game, played by people, making one move and then another in a lifespan, but always played according to strict rules which, in this case, are set within the steel frame and the rigging points. Again, it is noncompositional, and like a sail boat it performs and looks as well regardless of how the sails may be set or what tack it is taking.

Plug in and Clip on: Interchanging the Parts

Sometimes, though not often, architects have the opportunity to persuade clients that permutative devices may be in their own best interest, even though that client or his professional program writer has neglected it. I had such an opportunity in carrying out the commission for a library and educational resource building for Staten Island Community College in 1974. The New York State Dormitory Authority had no requirement for phased construction, future growth, or changing use. However, the building complex was developed so that separate basic fixed elements could be built in phases and connected at various levels by bridges, with footings attached to short columns set for future additions. To these fixed elements of concrete construction could be attached many small, enclosed elements, that is, seminar rooms, faculty offices, and carrels, whose position would not be fixed or actually

determined for the present or in the future. A system was developed whereby all these small elements were designed as light steel frame and steel clad boxes to be clipped on the periphery at any or all levels of the basic concrete elements. "Clipped on" is a glib statement, when in reality we had to design not only prefabricated boxes with lift points for crane handling, but attachment points for structural connection to any position on the periphery of the concrete frame. In addition, we arranged for tapping into a peripheral service distribution system to provide hot and chilled water for air conditioning units, telephone, intercom, and power for each of these boxes. Although we met construction budgets, won the final acceptance of a reluctant client, and secured the approval of the New York City Building Department whose standards we met, construction was delayed due to changes in educational policy. However, since we proceeded through working drawings with the building, we are able to speak with authority and assurance that a building that can truly be changed is no longer an impractical

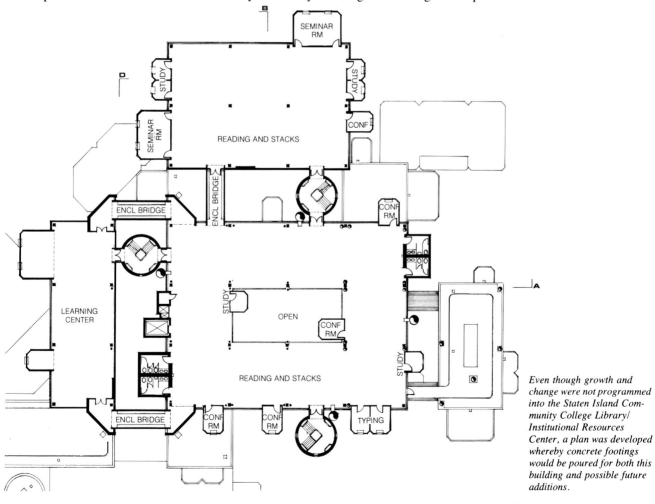

Even though growth and change were not programmed into the Staten Island Community College Library/ Institutional Resources Center, a plan was developed whereby concrete footings would be poured for both this building and possible future additions.

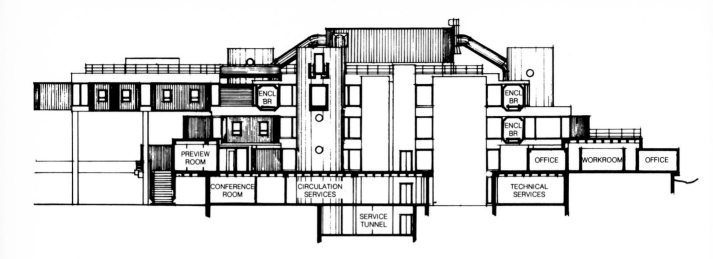

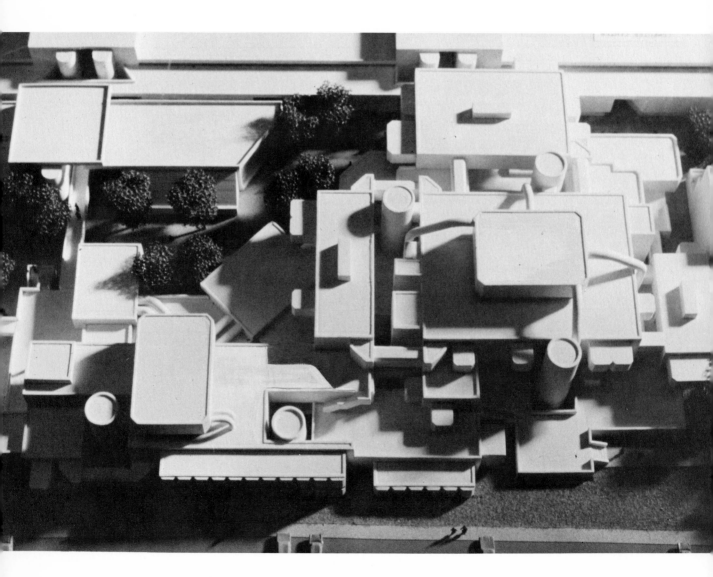

dream. It can be realized within current technologies without paying a premium.

The issues involved in this project can be summed up as follows: first, the life patterns of an academic community; second, a program of potential human needs to be assembled; third, an analysis of what is static as opposed to what may grow, change, or no longer be relevant; fourth, the technical devices by which change and growth can be accommodated; and fifth, the aesthetic or poetic qualities to be discovered in all the above and expressed in the final architectural realization. These issues all revolve about process. Behind all phenomena of nature is process. And for the architect to design, not by the Beaux Arts principle of "the tasteful arrangement of compositional elements," but through an understanding of processes, is not only to better accommodate man's physical needs, but to bring him closer to himself and to the nature of which he is a part. This provides perhaps a sixth, philosophical issue.

Kinetics: Moving the Parts

Taking the idea of change or movement further, another dimension to achitecture is kinetics. We are now able to satisfy that basic fascination with movement, not by illusion, as in the Baroque period, but with the technology we now command, producing buildings which, in part, do indeed move. As the history of architecture bears out, most innovations are drawn from either humble or crude and vulgar utilitarian origins. The barrel vault and arch were known to the Egyptians and Greeks, who used them only for underground sewage, whereas the Romans and others for centuries later got a lot of mileage out of them. Hidden steel tension structures, which used to hold Renaissance domes from collapsing, have now come to be commonly exposed. Kinetic devices first appeared in industrial buildings in the form of such things as attached hoists, overhead conveyors, power scaffolding, pneumatic tube intercom, trackage, and self-erecting cranes. Now when an improved service is performed, sooner or later an architect will make it somehow publicly acceptable on an aesthetic level. Increasingly there appear kinetic devices, vividly expressed, in airports, supermarkets, and flashy hotels. Kinetics is here—to perform greater service and to delight in.

Except for the most usual moving elements such as elevations, I have not yet designed a kinetic building. However, following the sequence of my works and with my continuing interest in an architecture of parts, it is with kinetics that I now come face to face. And as the house as building type is always a good proving ground, I sketched in 1960 a house of parts which could be assembled and disassembled on railroad trackage. A central element containing the entrance, living room, kitchen, bath, power source, had other parts, such as master bedroom, guest room, studio, and a "folly or mood room," grouped around it. For the practicalities of domestic life, or for reasons of pure whim, this house's functional grouping could be changed by sliding one or another of the elements along the tracks. From an aesthetic point of view, this house is never a static composition, but enters that field of experience now limited to kinetic sculpture.

Required frequency of change and movement have much to do with the design of the moving element. In the domestic area, changes in family life cycle are gradual and movement infrequent. Seasonal adjustments governed by weather are more frequent, while daily requirements involving daytime and nighttime uses are still more so. Then there are motivations of whim, the psychological need for change, and the sheer amusement in seeing things move.

In any case, I believe kinetics is more and more a part of our lives. The fusion of transportation and the building, people-moving devices, theater technology, museum and exhibition display, the opening and closing of solar-heated buildings, all these current developments confirm the functional justification of movable parts. The public's delight in the exposed machinery of the Roosevelt Island cable car system, the exposed elevator cabs in the Portman hotels, the scenic railroad entering the hotel lobby in Orlando's Disney World, and now the super-Mannerists growing involvement with changeable facades and room liners confirm the aesthetic acceptance of kinetics as well.

The most important element in architecture, however, is still "the part." The part appears, first, in analysis of the program; then, in synthesis, in the typing of parts; then, in the grouping of parts—assembly, rigging, interchange, reshuffling—and, finally, in movement. This seems to be the basis of my ordering devices and organizing ideas. The vivid expression, articulation, detailed connections, and couplings are the poetic touches I give in the design process, thereby possibly making something more of problem solving and building technology. If I add my other concerns to this—our sense of life, our basic psychological motivations, newly awakened perception of the impact of our electronic age, and our historic derivations—I hope to come up with something which can be called architecture.

Opposite page, top: At the Staten Island Community College Library/Center the prefabricated boxes had to be designed in such a way as to be easily erected by cranes and easily attached or detached from both the structure and the servicing.

Opposite page, bottom: The model of the Library/Center shows the circular core elements, the main functional elements, and the clipped-on parts.

FUMIHIKO MAKI

Born in Tokyo in 1928, Fumihiko Maki received his Bachelor of Architecture from the university there in 1952. He then went to America to study at the Cranbrook Academy of Art and earned a Master of Architecture in 1953. The next year he acquired still another degree, this one a Master of Architecture from Harvard. He worked for Skidmore, Owings & Merrill and Sert/Jackson before teaching, first at Washington University in St. Louis and then at Harvard. He has been teaching periodically since then at universities throughout the world.

Maki first stepped into the international spotlight in 1960 when he became a member of the Metabolist group. Inspired by Kenzo Tange's plan for Tokyo, the Metabolists were a group of architects who met to explore the future of architecture in Japan and produced a handbook for the World Design Conference of 1960. Maki's contribution was an article on the vernacular aesthetic of hill towns; it was an "attempt to create a total image of the vitality of group while retaining the identity of individual elements." Several years later, Maki published his Investigations in Collective Form, *in which he synthesized and developed these ideas. Since then he has published an article entitled "Movement Systems in the City" where he argues the importance of incremental processes of built forms in existing cities, using various modes of movement systems as vehicles of such transformations.*

Maki's work has been called "contextural" because of his obvious interest in developing systems which are coherent in themselves as systems and also part of a larger urban whole. This is typified by such buildings as Hillside Terrace Housing, which is notable for its hierarchy of public, semipublic, and private spaces and volumetric vistas strung along a pedestrian circulation mall. Maki has always felt that the architect must design buildings to fit into the larger whole, and that technology must be a servant of human need. His search for industrialized components out of which to construct buildings that marry the best of industrialization with an appropriate scale are a part of this belief. It is something that he is still in the process of developing.

View of the Central Building at Tsukuba University inside the gateway looking at the bris soleil, which doubles as a fireman's access. A steel element is used to turn the corner and articulate the structure.

Architecture has concerned itself with the creation of monumental forms in both the Western world and Japan until very recently. In the past few years there has been a turnabout from this way of thinking. We are now witnessing a resurgence of awareness of the human scale, the touchable scale, or the detail.

Amidst the gracious entrances and exits of such historical forces upon architecture, there are certain tenets which to me remain simple and timeless: not a steadfast adherence to a style or the excessive dependence on intellectualized concepts which tend to impose and dictate, but rather an attitude, and a relatively humble one at that, of how spaces ought to be made.

I am very concerned with seeking a rapport between environment and building, between building and program, and between building and the parts from which it is constructed. It is not aphoristic to want to draw sensitively on the rich resources of the ineradicable but endlessly varied reality of the setting, taking from and then giving to it. This is the architect's conversation: a communication between his or her inner landscape and the specific conditions of a part of the world's landscape he or she is to deal with at that particular moment in time. Each project the architect undertakes is a conversation among the unique situation, the ever-increasing range of material and technical resources available, and the architect's ability to draw on the whole of these resources, which, among other things, include much of the world's inherited knowledge, traditions, racial culture, and philosophies.

I mentioned the "inner landscape" of an architect. This refers to the internationalized landscape of each person's sphere over time and space, culture and aspirations, and is basically what the architect has to offer. Thus equipped, I believe poetry in architecture will arise not by forcible application of a theoretical notion, but in the loving treatment of each design problem in its given sphere to create buildings that can exist comfortably within their physical or cultural environment while, at the same time, displaying an integrity and identity of their own.

Since architecture by its very nature is the art of constructing, one might seek a poetry in the way that buildings are put together. With the advent of the assembly line and the mass production ethic, people concerned with the changing nature of architectural problems face a new challenge in the possibilities offered by prefabrication and industrialization of buildings. One wonders whether the same principles which had so successfully produced motor cars and refrigerators can be lifted whole and transposed directly into architecture or whether some sort of editing process is in order. The niche for prefabrication in architecture seems to reside in mass housing projects, where the mere quantity of repetitive units warrants standardization. In other projects where unique conditions dictate individualized design solutions, designing prefabricated components for their own sake may require more than clever maneuvers to gain some very attractive reductions in cost or even assembly efficiency. If one is not careful, it may also be easy to enslave design to a theoretical economy,

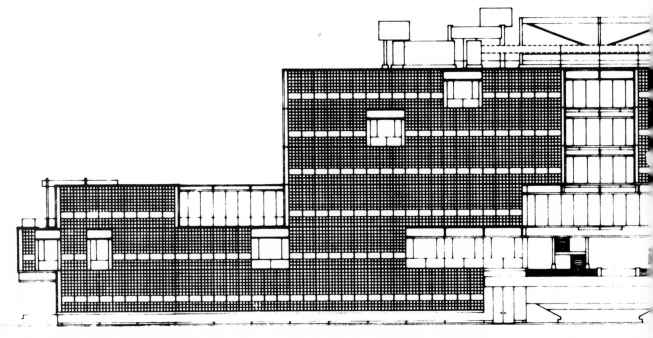

for standardization is a process that depends on quantity production and uniform conditions in both physical situations and market demand. Even though the danger of monotony, if not the inhumanity of mindless repetitions of a so-called universal solution, is inherent in the nature of standardization, there are certain things that one can achieve with prefabricated units even in unique situations that the more conventional construction methods cannot offer. Industrialization of construction components has long existed. One finds well-used catalogs of window frames, wall panels, electrical equipment, air conditioners, and so on lining the architect's bookshelves. It is only the degree to which prefabrication dominates a design that has changed over time.

We have long accepted the industrial product in architecture. But it is how one seeks out the special sweetness of those products as suited to the specific conditions of the problem and how one uses those special qualities to serve one's attitude in design that is the important issue for me.

Somewhere in each of the three projects I am going to touch on, the unique conditions called for the proficiency of a quick assembly system, and in each case I drew on the technical resources of prefabrication to produce a rather interesting marriage between the program and the design solution. As I find delight in the mellow humanness of the handmade scale and I also derive pleasure out of exploiting the potential of industrialized elements at an appropriate scale, we generated a prefabricated unit of intermediate scale for each of these three recently completed buildings. The typical prefabricated building element is usually small, giving the building the characterless appearance of being many, many identical or nearly identical pieces bolted together. One-of-a-kind design solutions, however, tend to be economically impractical in all but the most extravagant commissions. The intermediate scale is a way of trying to have the best of both worlds.

The thought process in such cases is not necessarily linear. From the germinal idea of using prefabricated units to facilitate assembly, there was constant interplay between the designs of the prefab element and the building as a whole. It is hard to distinguish or to delineate between cause and effect in the series of interdependent design decisions. The total effect of each project is partially a function of the prefab units, which in turn are partially a function of the nature of each project. The elements possess special potential, which was explored and integrated into the aesthetics of the project conditions. "Prefabrication" elicits an image of coarse-grained expansiveness, but here three different sets of conditions tailored some very individualized elements that serve the designs, while possessing the qualities of safety and efficiency of assembly which inspired the architects in the first place.

Central Building at Tsukuba University

The "out-and-out curtain wall," as the facade of the Central Building at Tsukuba University has

The Central Building gateway leads to the Tsukuba University campus. Since this was one of the first buildings at the university, the building is also a kind of gateway. Behind the large window are the student lounges and meeting areas.

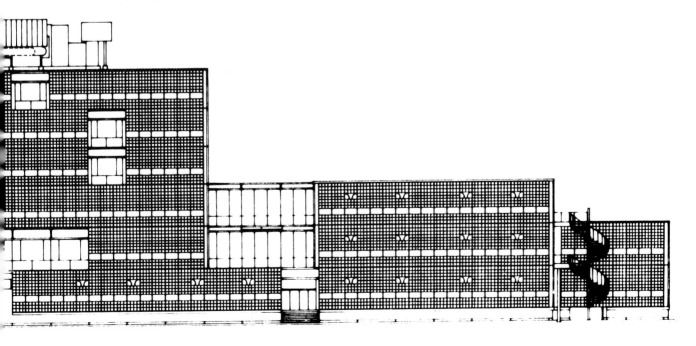

been described, is a composition of three prefabricated panel types: one with an operable, horizontal, transparent window near its base; one with two; and a third with a circular vent in a glass block plane. Together they clad the exterior of the building while allowing natural light to filter into the inside spaces of the art and physical education departments they house. Glass blocks are used throughout on the southern and northern facades. On the inside, they extend from the ceiling to eye level, where a window of transparent glass is placed horizontally, framing a view of the outside. Then the translucent blocks continue to the floor level and below. A clear amber tone, which varies slightly at different times of day, was made especially for these blocks. The warm amber filtered light was one effect we aimed at, vaguely reminiscent of paper shoji screens. The translucency of the wall vocabulary is echoed in the larger scale by the spatial treatment of the outside and the inside of the building. A central well sheltered by a hovering steel roof defines and protects a series of meeting spaces and intersections of traffic, an inside outside, which in a way is also translucent.

Here we attempted an architectural expression based on light and walls, experimenting with this through the use of prefabrication. I was interested in a new, more efficient way of handling a delicate material, the glass block, to which, incidently, one can easily become addicted. We were especially concerned with the insulation, luminosity, and strength of the panels. Since this was an experiment and because Japan has a history of earthquakes, I made sure to repeatedly test the panels against torsion in anticipation of stresses which might be caused by the earthquakes.

The translucent blocks were set into steel frames that measure about 4 by 10 feet (1.2 by 3 meters). The frames were fully fabricated, with the glass blocks and windows in place, and then the sections were raised up for installation. Steel framing and floor decking, poured concrete, lightweight steel studs, and cast aluminum panel partitions completed the structural language. In all, there were few materials and the method of construction was made simple and fast through basic patterns and frames which can be combined and recombined to form spaces appropriate to the specifics of the program.

Assembly on site was relatively uncomplicated. Whole panels were hoisted up and slip joined into the main structure. It took only a few installations for the workers to tune into the assembly techniques, and then the job proceeded quite elegantly, taking practically no time at all.

Opposite page: The southern facade of the Central Building at Tsukuba University shows the combination of the three basic panel types. The cost of this wall is comparable with that of a normal curtain wall.

Left: Joining the panels to the structure was a very delicate problem as the joint had to be strong enough to keep water out and flexible enough to expand and contract with changes in temperature so as not to transmit forces from the structure to the panels.

The predetermined dimensions of the panels were large enough to be recognizable as units and at the same time small enough to be easily joined to the building. They also allowed us to articulate the gateway to the future university and mountain range beyond, perforations in an aesthetic generated from their own logic. But because the old hand-laying method was not employed, the resulting facade has a contemporary quality to it.

The Okinawa National Aquarium

The Okinawa National Aquarium was the principal building for the Fish Cluster in the International Ocean Exposition of 1975. Built in the subtropical climate of Okinawa, the building's arcade—a significant part of the program— provides shade from the brutal sun for the people waiting to see the aquarium inside. The necessity for relatively quick construction suggested that a prefabricated element be developed. In this case, precast concrete components in the shape of a quadrant of a circle are detailed to form the structure of the arcade around the aquarium periphery as well as provide a major expressive element in

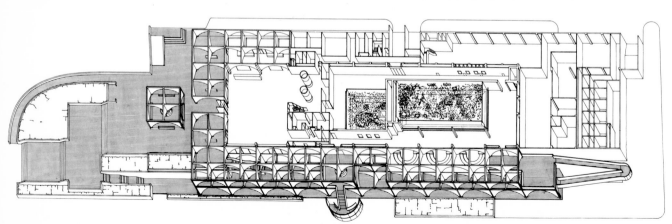

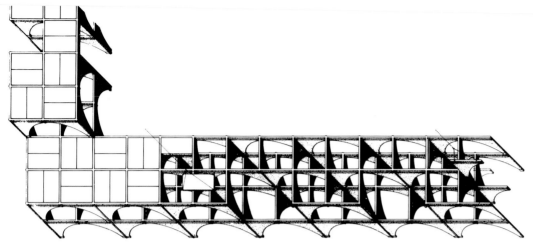

Opposite page, top: Overview of the Okinawa National Aquarium. On the right are two steel arches from which are suspended a tensile structure made out of a fisherman's net. This gives shade to the people watching the dolphins perform while picking up the semicircular forms of the arcades.

Opposite page, bottom: This axonometric shows the interweaving of the precast concrete arcades with the long-span steel hybrid structure of the central part of the building.

Top: The precast system works both vertically and horizontally; each unit with its 12 parts took a day to erect. It is possible to continue this system for several more stories either by thickening the concrete of the bottom arcs or by varying the reinforcing inside.

Bottom: Some of the precast units are placed outside the building enclosure to form an arcade, which provides shade for people queuing up in the tropical heat.

Above: At the Okinawa National Aquarium the world's largest fish tank is enclosed by eight layers of plastic, which comprise each 9-in. (22.9-cm) thick panel and are cantilevered from below. Instead of conventional steel mullions, the joints between the panels are neoprene so that people can see the totality.

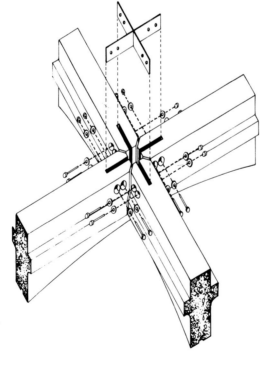

Right: The precast concrete joint at the apex of the arches. Since the structural system is a three-hinged arch, minimum moment is transmitted between the members. This system of bolting is simple enough for unskilled laborers to handle on the site.

Far right: Each roof panel has a quarter circle secondary beam in it; four of them make a complete circle, which is consistent in expression with the circular forms of the arcade. This kind of expression can only be done effectively through the use of prefabrication.

and outside the main spaces of the building.

The steel frames of the precast concrete components were designed and made in the mainland of Japan. They were then shipped to a temporary factory in Okinawa where concrete was precast to make those units. Besides shortening construction time, prefabrication eliminated the need for skilled labor, which was scarce in the Okinawa region at that time.

The structural system involves two kinds of elements. The first, 16′ by 10′ by 10″ (4.8 m by 3 m by 25.4 cm) concrete arcs, combines the functions of post and beam. Two such elements form a three-hinged arch; twelve of them make up a complete unit. This three-hinged arch transmits minimal moments at the joints, making them simpler to assemble. It is possible to repeat the system vertically and horizontally. On top of the arches rests the second kind of element, the ribbed floor or roof slabs. The rib takes the form of a quarter circle. Four of these 8 by 16 foot (2.4 by 4.8 meter) slabs form a complete circle. Both kinds of elements may be combined in diverse ways. With a minimum number of different elements, a great number of arrangements are possible.

A total of nearly 300 post and beam units and 150 floor/roof slabs were used. They were combined by means of dry joints. Bolting, the simplest and most primitive method of connection, was used because it requires no skilled labor. After the

pieces were fabricated in the temporary factory, they were ready for erection. Just before the time of assembly, the pieces were transported by trucks to the construction site where they were hoisted into place and connected.

By producing changing patterns of light and shade, the arcades punctuate and vary the scale of what, without them, would be a bulky mass. These raw concrete elements, coated with a clear acrylic spray, are juxtaposed against deep brick infill facade walls, forming cool strong shadows, while simultaneously framing views of the blue ocean and sky for those who care to nestle into their recesses. Most important, they provide shade, which is very much needed in the scorching Okinawa summers.

The variations produced by those very simple forms would have been difficult to create without appearing contrived if conventional methods of pouring concrete were employed.

Osaka Prefectural Sports Center

Built in a long, narrow industrial belt of reclaimed land beside a shoreline fronting a public canal, the Osaka Prefectural Sports Center faces a nondescript gray postwar residential sprawl in the Osaka City suburb. Its profile was conceived as an indi-

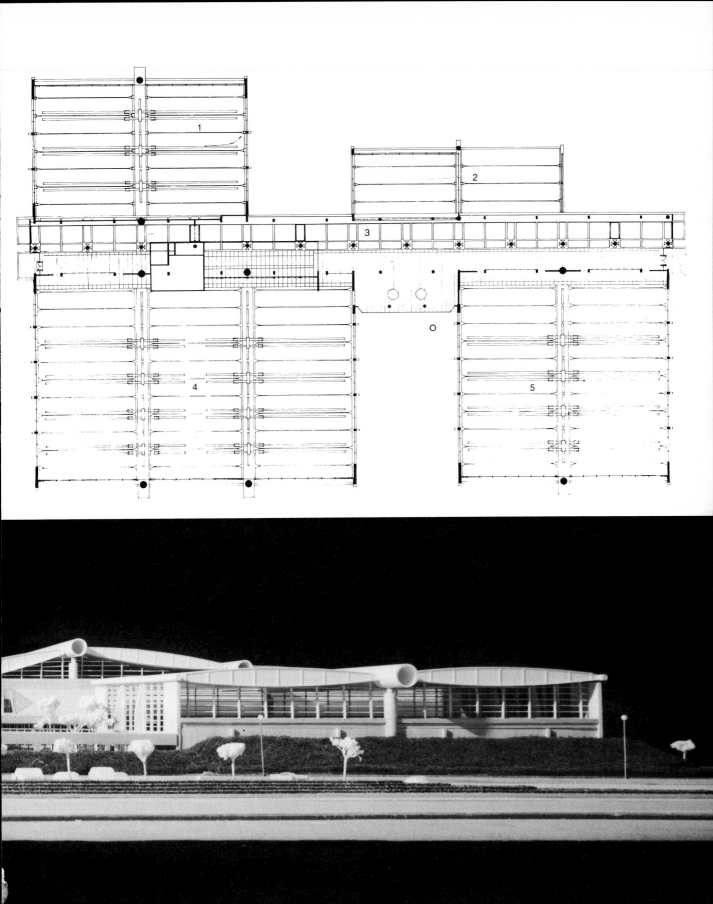

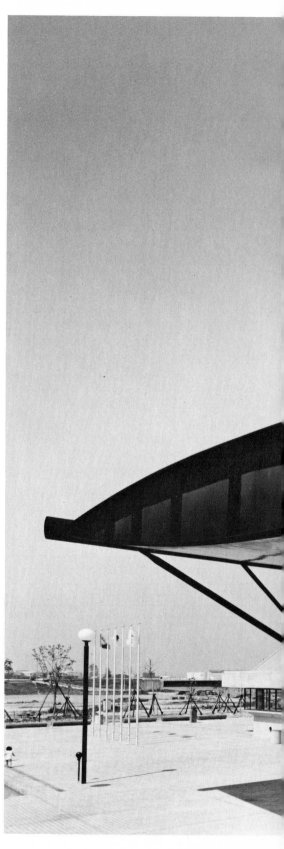

Top: While the structure of the Osaka Prefectural Sports Center is being erected, panels are being assembled on the ground nearby.

Above: It took only 16 days to install all 88 roof panels.

Right: At the entry a weathering steel plate was used instead of a net on the underside of the panels. The angle of these panels was inverted to heighten the sense of entry.

*Roof of the swimming pool/
skating rink of the Osaka Prefectural Sports Center shows
the integration of the structural, mechanical, and spatial systems.*

vidualized transition between them. The plan is organized along a circulation spine, with the major spaces staggered on both sides. These include a main gymnasium for basketball, volleyball, and other indoor sports; an indoor swimming pool that can be used as a skating rink in winter; a subgymnasium; communal facilities; lobbies; administration offices; and a restaurant. We wanted it to be a district nucleus with an intimate, approachable image. Hence, besides the large-span spaces, we tried to create an identity for the entry and, as far as possible, for the other spaces as well.

I developed prefabricated pieces for the roofs as a unifying but intermediate scale element. These roofing units consisted of spindle-section and rectangular-section trusses bound together to form large, unified panels. There were 88 sections in all. Each measured 10 by 70 feet (3 by 22 meters) in cross section and was covered by thin weathering steel plates as exterior protection against the polluted environment. The underside of the spindle-shaped unit was covered with a metal net and penetrated by secondary ducts feeding into the major ducts and the 140-foot (42-meter) long, 9-foot (2.7-meter) deep exhaust duct which acted as a major girder for these units.

The spindle-shaped pieces formed the intermediate-scale prefabricated components and the unifying vocabulary of the whole. While the major skeleton of the sports center was being built, these roof units were assembled simultaneously on the ground. Each truss was combined with its subducts, lighting fixtures, and ceiling. They were lined up on the ground, joined, and prepared to be hoisted up when the primary skeleton was complete. A row of spindle-section units joined laterally was attached perpendicularly to the pipe girders to form part of the roof.

The angle at which each row meets the girder determines the pitch of that part of the roof, and was used as one of the means to differentiate and span the various large spaces within the program. Two such panels cover the main gymnasium, another three span the pool, two cover the smaller gymnasium, and two roof the entrance hall.

The main beams, placed strategically at the pinnacles formed by the junctures of the large panels, bear the load of the roof and transmit vertical compression, which is then absorbed by the pins and by deflection of the cylindrical posts. Formed of thick curved sheets, the main roof beams are hollow, like bamboo stalks. They are ribbed at fixed intervals and fitted with axial flow exhaust fans.

The use of intermediate-scale prefab units allowed efficient construction in a congested industrial zone. All units were factory produced, combined on the ground, and hoisted up to be installed, a process which took only 16 days.

The prefabricated pieces also allowed the large spaces to be gently scaled and, in a way, particularized on both the inside and the outside. The entry is given special articulation by a reverse curvature of those same panels of prefab units, opening up and out to project a welcoming approach. Over the administration areas the curve is neutralized, as opposed to the generous slopes over the swimming and the court spaces.

In all three projects we were looking for a way to create a unit element larger than a person, yet smaller than a room, which had a character of its own and which could be combined and permuted to respond to specific functional requirements. In addition we were interested in exploring the horizons of prefabrication, of industrialized building, in a way that might point out possibilities for the future. These buildings were efficient to erect, not costly, satisfied the programs, and did so in a poetic way.

GERALD MCCUE

Gerald McCue was born in 1928 and received a Bachelor of Arts degree from the University of California at Berkeley in 1951; he received a Masters in architecture a year later. He then entered practice and built a range of building types from private houses and subway stations to a marina and corporate headquarters. These works have earned over thirty design awards, including four national and seven regional American Institute of Architects honor awards. He has also conducted research, the most interesting and most recent of which are his studies concerning the effect of earthquakes on building components and ways of developing design procedures to accommodate earthquake hazards. This work has been published in a report, Architectural Design of Building Components for Earthquakes. He has also been interested in architectural programming and published a paper on that in 1978.

After having taught at his alma mater and serving successively as a lecturer, professor, and chairman, he moved to the Harvard Graduate School of Design, where he held the position of chairman of the architecture department and associate dean. Recently he was appointed dean of the school. McCue's conceptual concern with developing models for construction types without placing value judgments on any approach is a part of his concern about building well and building appropriately.

The exterior wall of the Alza Corporation Building shows a mix of homogeneous and heterogeneous enclosure conditions, as can be seen in the steel structure which is interwoven with the brick cladding material.

The modern era is not the first time that architectural design philosophies have been concerned with the process of building; however, most architectural periods have been characterized by concern for better ways to build and their appropriate visual expression. The design philosophies of the modern school have tended to celebrate the construction aspects of building. The most sought-after expression has attempted to establish the reality of a building by honestly and directly showing the nature of the structure, materials, and methods of assembly. Concerned with both the means of construction and its expression, this design philosophy has set high ideals; through the years, outstanding prototypes have established the validity of this philosophy and illustrated that architecture can reach a high level of technical and aesthetic elegance following these principles. But often the visual expression has been more powerful than the underlying philosophy. Many stylistically modern buildings have been built which emulate or exaggerate an assembled appearance, but do not derive their expression from logical construction processes. Other supposedly modern buildings have deviated even further from the basic design philosophy, seeking visual effects regardless of how ill-conceived the building may be as a constructed object. In these cases, the design principles relating to expression have become hollow and meaningless as they have been separated from the more basic philosophic principles relating to the advance of the construction aspects of building.

Expression of Construction in Architecture

Currently the intentions of the modern movement are being questioned and the design principles relating to expression are being challenged. Certainly one must concede that a large number of buildings styled in the modern manner do not express the integrity or the logic of construction which the design principles intended. To further the discussion, I will explore two themes here: why constructive expression is relevant and that the lack of appropriate conceptual models for linking the objectives for construction with the objectives for expression is one cause for misuse of the design principles. Our concern for construction and the expression of that concern in the fabric of our buildings is only one of the many objectives of our design efforts. Often it is not the most important concern, but in varying degrees it always contributes to the overall expression. Our purpose here is to show that adherence to the basic philosophic intentions results in buildings with different architectural expressions for different situations, while the seeking of expression regardless of the situation results in stylistic mannerism.

It is useful to note that regardless of the designer's intentions buildings by their very nature are material constructs. Therefore, regardless of the relative emphasis one wishes to give to the means of construction, to some degree built form does impart the characteristics of what and how it is made. The issue for the designer is not whether this relationship exists, but given the relationship, at what level of expression do purpose, form, and constructive expression interact.

The levels at which we perceive and react to environmental settings provide an indication of the importance of how things are made. Normally, one comprehends the social setting, its symbolic content, the space and form, and the material expression in approximately that hierarchical order. But to some degree, each embodies the other; they are symbiotic. Materials, and the way they are expressed, have both formal and symbolic content; they are important to our perception and to our understanding of the environment and are capable of imparting an added level of meaning to both form and setting.

Dada and other movements in art have illustrated the strength of our expectations and associations among symbol, material, and purpose. Works of art and architecture have both congruence and conflict between expectation and reality. In spite of the occasional shock value of conflicting associations, significant architecture normally embodies a high correspondence between the spatial and formal attributes and the material systems by which it is made. This belief should not be interpreted as support for constructivist exhibitionism in form or material. Rather, I believe that there is an appropriate material, construction, and expression which provides meaning to form in a particular setting. In this respect, the level of appropriateness is determined by the nature of the form-making task to be accomplished as well as its relation to functional and symbolic intent. Thus, for buildings where merely achieving the enclosure is a technological feat, the dominance of structural forms may enhance the meaning of the form and its expression. In contrast, the same level of structural dominance for achieving a relatively simple space or form may be inappropriate and actually destructive to either the form or the social setting. Both formal condition and social conditions as well as formal context should therefore influence the overall material and construction vocabulary.

Architecture reaches greatness when there is strong interaction with—but not necessarily formal congruence between—activity systems and space-form and where there is a high degree of correspondence among—but not necessarily slavish consistency among—form, material, and means of construction. Many architects have demonstrated these principles as part of their concern for what might be called building well. Directness of form and expression in relation to construction often flows naturally from an understanding of how to build.

A Homogeneous Model

Conceptual models play an essential part in applying more abstract values in design. It is useful to digress for a moment and explore what appear to be deficiencies in the prevalent conceptual models. Early in the modern movement it became apparent that there were two relatively new material systems which could satisfy the objective for advanced technology and enhance a directness of expression: concrete frames and exposed steel frames. Masonry bearing walls would have met the criteria for expression, but they were antithetical to the technological pretensions of the movement. As a result, the concrete of Le Corbusier and the steel of Mies proved most legitimate and provided the prototypical examples which were to be the primary influences on design philosophy.

Unfortunately, the design philosophy has not provided coherent conceptual models of how to build, permitting what would have the more abstract objectives to be achieved in situations where the prototypes did not fit. Rather than a philosophy of construction which serves the designer, there have been only type solutions, which are not applicable in many real situations.

One may validly criticize modern architecture for becoming obsessed with superficial visual effects which become mannerisms, rather than being concerned with a deeper philosophy which permits evolution. This has often led to a decadence of architectural expression, as the superficial visual characteristics of the prototypes have been copied and recopied so that they are often perverted in both material and form. Just as in the neoclassical buildings that the modern movement was to replace, there is often little correlation currently between what buildings appear to be and how they are made. For instance, Miesian frames and walls move from inside to outside, changing environmental materials as they penetrate the environmental skin; or similarly, Corbusian concrete-derived forms are fabricated from other materials, including masonry, wire-mesh, and plaster.

Most conceptual models used for the design are essentially structural rather than environmental. As a result they do not adequately fit the complexity of the modern building task and, therefore, fail to provide the proper theoretical framework for achieving appropriate levels of correspondence between form and means. The conceptual model represented by Le Corbusier's domino formed an important tenet of the modern movement; the introduction of bending through slab and columns and later through frames liberated modern architecture from the formal restrictions imposed by earlier compression-only load-bearing systems. As prototypes emerged in concrete and steel, this model presented a conceptual basis for relating structure and form, but did not adequately address environment and form. It is a ''homogeneous model'' where an ideal building is one in which the structure and finish are materials which are ideally homogeneous; at the very minimum, the materials must be suitable for exposure both inside and outside the building. In this conceptual model, glass is not a form-defining material, but a nonmaterial which can be located anywhere within the structure without affecting the essential characteristics. In this concept there is no real distinction between interior and exterior space; materials define form in a similar manner whether inside or outside.

This concept borrows from what we admire about earlier architectural periods: the brick forms of Roman baths and basilicas or the forms of the Gothic cathedrals. It also draws from the more primitive vernacular buildings where space was often formed with the same materials inside and out. Considered environmentally, this model derives most of its characteristics from buildings in warm moderate climates where there is little significant environmental difference between interior and exterior spaces in terms of either social separation of activities or climatic separation for environmental control. One of the important features of this conceptual model is that by moving doors and glass in and out within this homogeneous structure, one may retain a consistency of both formal and material expression.

There is a natural expressive appeal to this model. It is understandable, it permits powerful and free sculptural forms, and it provides legitimate deep modeling of space. Its prototypical examples provide powerful visual images, but they have often been perverted when built in social settings or with material systems inconsistent with the imperatives of this concept.

From among our work the Chevron industrial process research laboratory designed in 1966 for

Opposite page: Located adjacent to the oil refinery, the Chevron Laboratory is constructed out of concrete to avoid unnecessary fireproofing and finishes as well as to keep the structure and servicing clean and exposed as part of the organizational concept. Because the requirements are so huge, the primary air supply system is located in the horizontal manifolds in the front of the building.

Top: On the other side, the main facade is expressed by the precast concrete vertical exhaust ducts.

Bottom: Detail of the exhaust ducts shows the change in texture between the precast ducts and the rest of the cast-in-place concrete.

the Standard Oil Company of California in Richmond, California, comes closest to the homogeneous model. The cast-in-place concrete frame and precast exterior infill walls maintain the same form, material, and finish inside and out. Supported on clusters of deep driven wooden piles, the vertical structure consists of concrete piers supporting longitudinal girders with transverse beam and slab floors. The typical section consists of long span floor beams with cantilevers on each side. A little unusual in concrete construction, the floor girders and beams are in different horizontal planes like conventional wood construction, to permit through access for utilities in each axis. While the structure was cast-in-place, nonstructural elements of the exterior including both infill walls and the air ducts are of precast concrete.

The frame as a whole has its own visual integrity; definition of interior and exterior space is achieved by moving glass or infill panels into different positions within the frame. Exposed utilities were a programmatic necessity and main-

tained a consistent expression of this model. The utilities, like the structure, move inside and outside, exposed in both locations. The few interior finishes are carefully set off by reveals or by the concrete systems of the frame, never penetrating to the exterior. Consistent with this model, the ground floor was paved inside and out.

At a detail level of expression, both concrete systems of the Chevron Laboratory express how they were made: the cast-in-place concrete was formed with rough sawn boards, the precast in reusable forms. In retrospect, the offset in plane between the two systems seems unnecessary as the change in surface texture and articulation of joints provide sufficient distinction between the two processes. The overstatement of the assembly aspects of construction was destructive to the more basic formal definition; an articulated joint would have sufficed to define the material systems and yet maintain continuity of form.

After ten years, the techtonic expression of the Chevron Laboratory still seems reasonable for its use, its setting and its form. Since the mechanical systems are a meaningful part of the activities conducted there, their strong influence on the overall expression seems logical and appropriate. In some respects this building is environmentally simplistic, as befits the homogeneous model. The exposed structure penetrating from inside to outside without either moisture barrier or thermal isolation is only possible where there is no problem of a freezing line within members, where heat loss is not considered severe, and where interior and exterior fireproofing requirements are similar. The exterior concrete walls have neither insulation nor vapor barriers, but even in this particular climatic location, the lack of vapor barriers has created problems. In this mild climate the building was considered a reasonable solution, but where it has deficiencies they are due to its adherence to a structural, rather than an environmental, conceptual model.

A Heterogeneous Model

Other building purposes, other environmental settings, or other construction techniques may make the homogeneous model an inappropriate design. Considered only from an environmental point of view, one might take an entirely opposite approach where there is absolute differentiation between the interior and exterior environment—a "heterogeneous model." In this concept the building is considered to be bounded by layers which form the definition between interior and exterior spaces. Interior spaces, forms, and material systems have an integrity of their own and interact, but are not necessarily congruent, with the form and material systems of the boundary layer. Here, glass creates part of the boundary; it may be treated as an interruption in the primary material or as an integral part of a boundary surface of the skin. Followed consistently, the heterogeneous model leads to a totally different vocabulary of sculptural forms and establishes different disciplines of material use than the homogeneous model.

Historic and vernacular antecedents for the heterogeneous model are many, ranging from the Baroque churches with their severe granite facades revealing interiors of white and gold plaster to the layered walls of the so-called postmodernists. Buildings in northern regions with severe climates tend to support sharply different interior and exterior environments. Strong separations between interior and exterior social settings also tend to support this conceptual model as does construction where the materials of the fabric of the building are not suitable for exterior exposure.

IBM's Santa Teresa computer programming center near San Jose, California, designed in 1977, is one of the several projects we have completed which are variations of the heterogeneous model. Projects that adhere to this concept range from wood and shingle-covered houses to concrete and metal-clad institution buildings. They may look superficially different due to their forms and the particular material used for the boundary layer, but they are all essentially of the heterogeneous type and, therefore, belong to the same conceptual model. In many respects, these buildings result from pragmatic necessity, where dictates of either program or budget make it logical or essential to have structural or finish systems on the interior which are not suitable for exposure on the exterior. To follow this logic, the exterior boundary materials should not extend into the interior.

The IBM center houses offices for the programmers and their computer-support areas. All the interior space has been built as adaptable loft space and is currently subdivided into office cubicles finished with inexpensive interior finish materials; none of these materials penetrate the boundary to the exterior of the building. The steel moment-resisting structural frame was also fireproofed with interior finish materials. In this case, the boundary layer is a sheer surface skin; glass and aluminum panels are both treated as part of this skin, and these materials do not penetrate the boundary into the interior of the building. Consistent with this model, the boundary layer itself is heterogeneous; the outside aluminum surface is backed by vapor barriers and insulation and faced on the interior with the interior wall finish. It should be mentioned that development of the exterior curtain wall also represents a technological response to seismic design criteria.

At the ground level, the IBM project is also consistently heterogeneous. There are no sculptural penetrations which imply a deep wall boundary layer, but rather the expression is an admission of the thin surface skin. An illusion of modeling and penetration of space is accomplished, but through other means; the exterior walls and the interior walls of the core are layered pierced walls, defining a series of corridors which describe and link the workspace pavilions. Thus when moving through and around the project, a sculptural spatial feeling is achieved, which is entirely consistent with the heterogeneous model. The wall forms are made opaque through the use of mirror glass in the private office areas and transparent by clear glazing at the circulation corridors. The mirror glass is juxtaposed with intensive wall colors to cause the appearance of pene-

trations and spatial definition. Thus within the reflections, the design explores means for achieving space-form modeling which conveys deep volumes through means which are compatible with and which exploit the heterogeneous model.

A Composite Model

These two projects, the Chevron Laboratory and IBM's Programming Center, express literal translations of the polar extremes between the homogeneous and heterogeneous models. One model is not inherently better than the other, but each has its relevance and each may serve as a basis for developing an internally consistent logic for design development.

One of the deficiencies in the modern movement is the failure to identify legitimate conceptual models which meet real design conditions. The homogeneous model served as the ideal and gave many buildings built conditions which did not follow the underlying principle of the basic design philosophy. Consequently, architects often design buildings which have the essential characteristics of the heterogeneous model, yet attempt the aesthetic expression of the homogeneous form; the result is bastardization of form, material, aesthetic, and ethic.

A better understanding of these notions leads to conceptual models suitable for the particular purpose and environmental setting being addressed. An appropriate model will permit an approach to both overall formal issues and individual design details with a consistent theoretical frame of reference. Often conditions suggest a composite model which incorporates parts of both the homogeneous and heterogeneous models, where certain forms and material systems of the building fabric may serve inside and outside the environmental layer while others may not.

Designed in 1970, the Alza Corporation Building with pharmaceutical research space and headquarters offices in Palo Alto, California, is an example of the composite model. The requirements for long spans and the need for rapid erection led to selection of a steel frame for the structure. The ground floor is a concrete slab on grade; the second floor and roof are concrete fill on steel decking. The infill exterior walls are formed with precast concrete slabs welded by clips to the frame. The erection tolerances and procedures precluded a tight fit between slabs and steel; therefore, a waterproof membrane forming the actual environmental barrier was applied over the concrete and was flashed to the steel.

View on the garden level atop the IBM Programming Center looking at the office clusters. Each of the 2,000 offices in the complex is located along a private U-shaped corridor to maximize the number of perimeter offices. The exterior wall is one of the few walls ever specifically designed to be able to accommodate large lateral displacements during earthquakes. The aluminum panels are completely planar so that the plates of skin may rotate with respect to one another, while the corners will pop off in the event of a serious tremor.

This membrane was veneered with brick, applied in a clearly nonstructural manner. The building's small size permitted the steel skeleton to be exposed on the exterior without fireproofing, allowing the infill walls to be set in and out of the frame. In this respect, the building is homogeneous. However, the panels are obviously nonstructural and are so expressed by creating a deep wall solution. Glass is used in two ways: as non-wall in the deep wall areas and as part of the surface skin where the wall panels are set flush with the frame. It was not reasonable, however, to expose the steel girders on the interior, and therefore, the frame and infill panels are utilized as a deep wall environmental boundary.

One could argue that the composite model is a compromise solution, but that is not the case. As the Alza Building illustrates, it is reasonable to develop a boundary layer which has the characteristics of the homogeneous model yet clearly differentiates this layer from the interior of the building as in the heterogeneous model. In this case the exterior conveys the reality of how the building is made, and yet it does not seem incongruous to find more refined levels of finish on the interior. Because of the programmatic necessity for cleanliness and the social atmosphere of the activities, the utility services in the Alza laboratory are concealed in the more finished interior. Credibility of the concept is maintained by never allowing columns, structure, or ducting to appear on the interior and always exposing them in the boundary layer. Placing the environmental membrane back and forth within the deep walls proved difficult and expensive to build, however, and may be criticized for its lack of conceptual purity. While it was technologically feasible and there have been no problems, this is a slightly forced logic of expression.

This line of reasoning does not suggest that the designer should not choose to create interior spaces with essentially the character of exterior space, or vice versa. Contrast and ambiguity may be powerful ways of achieving overall objectives. But it does suggest that the conceptual model should be compatible with the problem at hand and with the realities of environmental separation that will exist; a definitive conceptual model provides a theoretical integrity for individual solutions.

Architectural design is the act of bringing together the what and how to build. The highest forms of architecture historically and presently are those which bring the functional and symbolic purposes of building into meaningful interaction with both the space form and the constructive

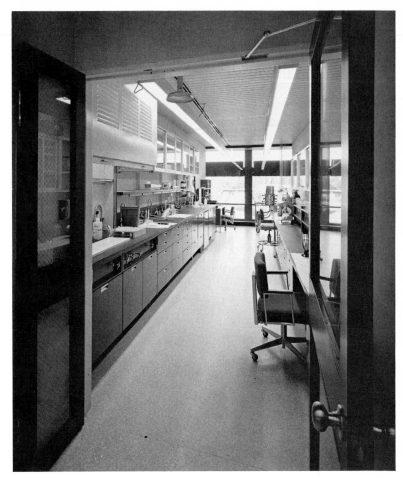

means of their achievement. If there is an inadequacy in modern architecture, it has been the superficial concern for expression rather than concern for broader principles. When visual and formal concerns become effects rather than an expression of both purpose and means, they lose the essential dimension of their meaning; buildings which are a collection of effects have little meaning.

Whether conscious to the designer or not, conceptual models of buildings as constructed objects are the basis for design decisions. One's design philosophy should not be wedded to the visual effect of a specific construction model, rather a model should be developed appropriate to the purpose, setting, and means of building. Consistent dedication to a philosophy which establishes conceptual models relevant to both the what and how to build provides the potential for new and creative expression with continued evolution and development, while architecture derived principally from expression often degenerates into mannerism.

Above: Despite the fact that the exterior wall zone is heterogeneous, the interior is very much a completely defined space.

Opposite page: The different environmental loads on the various faces of the Alza Corporation Building are reflected in the varying thicknesses of the walls: on the north facade, the structural and cladding elements are virtually flush, while on the west facade, they are split from each other.

RICHARD ROGERS

Richard Rogers was born in England in 1933. He received his Master of Architecture from Yale in addition to a few scholarships, including a Fulbright, which enabled him to study urban housing with Serge Chermeyeff. Following a brief stint with Skidmore, Owings & Merrill, to which some critics attribute his continuing interest in structural expression, he returned home to form his own firm in conjunction with his then-wife, Su, and Norman and Wendy Foster. TEAM 4, as it was called, began by building houses which were frequently submerged into their often spectacular sites. These houses were traditionally constructed out of modest materials. They also began building loose-fit structure-oriented solutions, highlighted by the Reliance Controls Factory in Swindon, England. About that time TEAM 4 dissolved, and Rogers began practicing with Renzo Piano, most noted as a designer of many geometrically innovative light-weight shell structures. During the twelve years they were together, Piano + Rogers produced a series of stunning loose-fit shed buildings constructed primarily out of standard off-the-shelf components borrowed from the automotive, shipbuilding, and aircraft industries. Putting a building together like an erector set, they have tried to seriously deal with technology as a source for answers to such problems as material scarcity and quality control of the construction process. They have thought a lot about growth and change, which materializes in their work in the flexibility of the open plan, the demountable partition, the interchangeable facade panel, and the ever-extensible extruded section.

Rogers has also taught extensively at places like Yale, UCLA, and MIT and won numerous competitions; the most recent is the new facility for Lloyds of London currently under construction and the most famous is, of course, Centre Pompidou.

Hung and strung with the paraphernalia of circulatory wizardry, Plateau Beaubourg is a kaleidoscopic jungle gym that all Paris can climb over, under, around, and through.

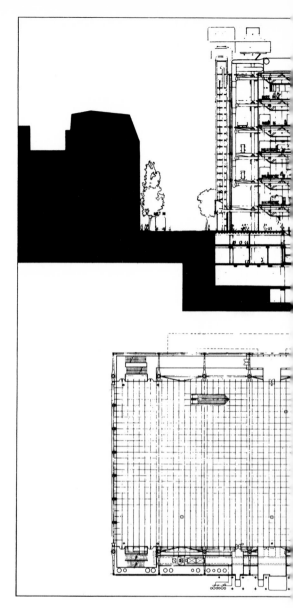

eaubourg was designed to be a live activity center, entertaining and informing the art historian, tourist, and neighboring Parisian, a place where all could participate in an urban, highly serviced machine, fluid and flexible, easy to change in response to changing needs. It was not to be a closed institution for the haves, but a place where activities are encouraged to overlap from street theater to the world's most refined acoustical laboratory. It was our belief that the more activities overlapped and enriched each other, the more likely it would be that exciting things would happen, opening up possibilities outside the normal confines of a cultural institution; the greater the public involvement, the greater the success.

The Design Concept

An architecture of possibilities is rooted in the constant of change. For in the dynamic and changing society in which we live, it is impossible to freeze time. Conceived as a flexible container capable of continuously adapting not only in plan, but also in section and elevation to whatever needs should arise, Plateau Beaubourg is an inside-out building. The 25-foot (7.5-meter) thick exterior structural wall zone houses the servicing entrails, movement galleries, and audiovisual information, while forming the structural cage which supports the five trays of column-free loft space. In addition to totally inverting the traditional notion of facade, it affords a technical simplicity by allowing components to be easily adapted, clipped-on, or removed. Beaubourg, constructed completely from prefabricated dry elements, becomes in essence a gigantic ever-changing erector set, as opposed to the more common doll's house with its precious, cosmetic, nonadditive, tailor-made detailing and its inherent lack of freedom and choice. The aim is to create a loose changeable framework with the economic precision of a watch mechanism in which people can freely participate. Their ever-changing activities both inside and outside the building give the construction a dynamic life, replacing the traditional static elevation, so that the building becomes the framework for live performances and not a cosmetic straightjacket. While the history of much of the modern movement has been one of flirtation with technology, it has always been somewhat superficial. We are trying to fully develop the theories of the pioneers, of such people as Wachsmann, Fuller, and Wright.

Flexibility is best illustrated in the partitioning system. Every partition is movable; the

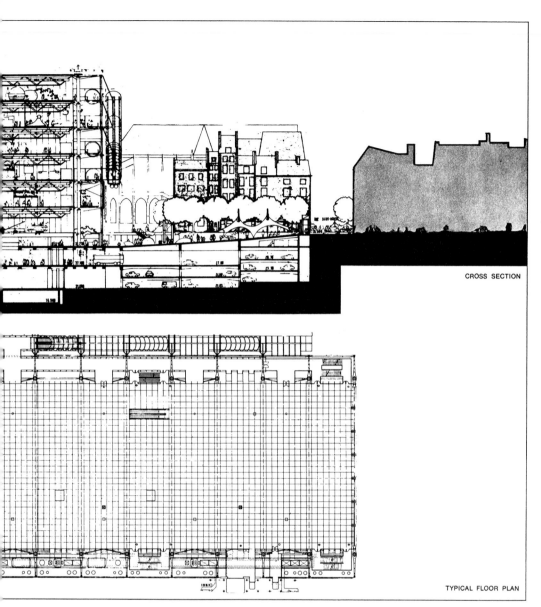

Beaubourg is a colossal cultural emporium, part British Museum, part Times Square, containing the normally disparate activities of a modern art museum, national reference library, industrial design center, and music/acoustic research facility. Rather than splitting the building into four watertight compartments, the Centre is a well-serviced shed consisting of five superimposed uniform spaces supported externally by a free-standing structural frame, the whole capable of change in plan, section, and elevation so as to accommodate the unforseen.

CROSS SECTION

TYPICAL FLOOR PLAN

Bürolandschaft office dividers can be shifted in a couple of minutes, the larger suspended museum partitions may take an hour, and the fire walls could require a day to unbolt. Even the facade is movable as it is free of the vertical structure. Should the situation require a more radical response, it is possible to completely gut the building down to the structure and begin over again.

There is another kind of flexibility in the building which is considerably more sophisticated and complex. It is most clearly shown in the Institute for Research and Coordination in Acoustics and Music, or IRCAM, which comprises one quarter of the program, the quarter located beneath the plaza. Here not only do the different studio types afford a complete range of volumetric options on which are superimposed a plethora of acoustical panels, but the largest studio/concert hall is designed to be continuously variable in both volume and acoustical qualities. Like the other studios, it has an acoustical chamber of double box construction; the outer shell is concrete and belongs to the primary structure, while the inner concrete box is isolated from it by soft rubber antivibration mounts. Little in the inner box is fixed, allowing the studio/concert hall ceiling to be split into three sections, each capable of moving 35 feet (11 meters) up or down; the resulting lateral gaps are filled in with acoustical curtains.

Each of the 180 motor-driven prismatic wall panels can be shifted into any one of seven possible positions. The floor is completely free and of platform construction (which is like a suspended ceiling except on the floor). The sound and light systems are highly sophisticated, enabling infinite configurations. Access to any part of the space is by ladders mounted on rolling transverse beams. Any combination of any parts is recorded on a computer so that it can be recalled at will.

Flexibility should be communicated by the legibility of a building. The people who are going to inhabit the space ought to be able to understand what is happening there and get some clues as to what they can do. One is constantly seeking universal rules so that one's design decisions do not stem purely from arbitrary preferences. To clarify the performance of the parts, we tend to separate their functions so that each part is no larger than absolutely necessary to do its work and plays a single role. Tension chords become the thinnest of solids, compression members are steel tubes; the differing diameters describe the various loads each member must carry. Each element is taken fully to its highest potential by the use of the most scientific means available. Likewise, every joint is univalent, articulated to enable easy erection and dissembling. To allow for control of quality,

Each part plays a single role and is optimally sized to perform its particular function. Every component and every joint is expressed.

cost, speed of erection, in addition to future change, industrial materials manufactured in controlled conditions are fully exploited. The building is truly a vast assemblage, a full-scale erector set—a concept which offers the design team a clear set of criteria for every detail and every connection. The architecture of Beaubourg becomes an expression of the process of building: the optimization of every single element, its system of manufacture, storage, transportation, erection, and maintenance all within a clearly defined and rational framework.

The Development of the Structure

Take, for example, the development of the primary structure. Because of the spans involved and the commitment to prefabrication, there was never any question of making the building in any material other than steel. As soon as it became apparent that there was a time constraint of five years from competition to opening, we realized that it would be utterly impossible to debug the initial idea of moving floors held by friction clamps in the time allotted and consequently abandoned it. The next development was right-angled verendale beams enclosed within floors and ceilings, which offered three totally clear floors sandwiched between alternate mechanical floors. Each beam was held between two pairs of double columns, a notion which turned out to be both inflexible and overweight. It also had an economic flaw: the beam should actually rest between the pairs of double columns so as to evenly distribute the load, which would force the beams to be 25 feet (7.5 meters) longer on each side than the final solution.

The structural solution finally adopted is simplicity itself. Descended from Gerber's 19th-century suspended bridge designs where the rotation of the moment arm is placed to coincide with the point of no moment, the superstructure is comprised of a suspended span with cantilever brackets. The trussed beams supporting the floors are pinned between the double row of compression columns, the geberettes hinged to their other sides. These in turn were laced together to resist wind, temperature, and horizontal and vertical forces. To take the lateral forces, the braced ends of the building form a gable frame. There are no expansion joints as all distortion forces are completely absorbed by the flexibility of the members or are resisted by their stiffeners; all pieces are, in other words, a little bit too short, forcing them into

tension. Astonishingly few members were required. Furthermore, the selection of the geberettes provided a golden opportunity to divorce the line of structure from the line of enclosure. This eliminated a special wall condition and fixed the facades. Hence, all infill elements are the same width and all interior partitions typical.

Though we had hoped to use standard components, the engineers soon proved that the scale of many of the parts was such that new techniques had to be developed to cut down on the amount of steel used. Advanced technology was, furthermore, the only way that it would be possible to achieve the volume of production necessary to meet the projected construction schedule. As usual this technology could be found more easily in the shipbuilding and aircraft industries, than in the building industry. So we turned to these industries for clues for steel casting techniques, for instance. Cast steel was chosen for the geberettes and all the nodes both for maximum economy of weight and as a way of expressing the form and detailing of the structure while establishing a method of maintaining strict control over the design as it developed. Because of the size and complexity involved in the production of the casting, it was a new venture for the building industry. Because it is impossible to weld the castings after completion, the way one can with ordinary steel, the technique also added a new constraint to the design team. All attachments had to be considered at the outset, long before the final heat treatment. It went well; the only problem turned out to be the brittle fracture of some of the geberette castings at the factory requiring the development of new backing procedures.

For less permanent needs, a secondary structural system was designed, ranging from the elevator towers to mezzanine supports to a framework for the ducts. As these are temporary in nature, the supports are constructed entirely out of standard steel components. These consist of a steel beam composed of simple channels with tubes for diagonals and steel columns made of four angles welded back to back. Both channels and angles are provided with holes to clip on additional components. Typical of the open-ended detailing of the secondary structure are the mezzanines. Intended to provide a movable intermediary floor, they are designed to be bolted to the trussed beams anywhere in the building, which did, of course, require that every beam be designed and built to carry them.

With the single exception of the columns which were brought to the site in halves and joined in mid-air, all structural elements were prefabricated

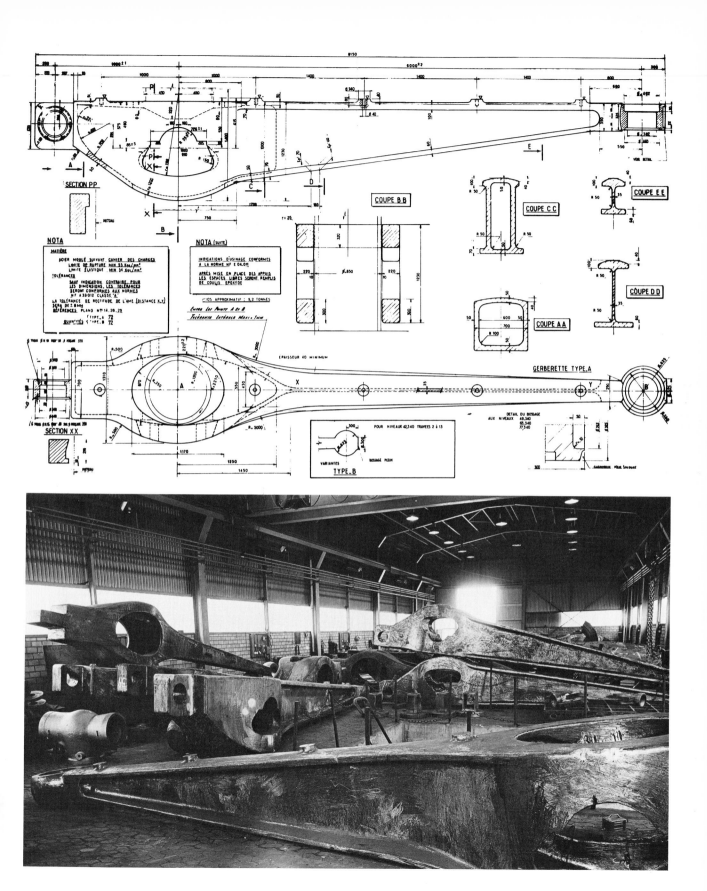

off-site to avoid site welding. By far the largest elements were the trussed beams measuring 148 feet (45 meters) in length and 10 feet (3 meters) in height and weighing 75 tons (67 metric tons). Every Thursday night the main steel contractors delivered three beams by special convoy. A single mobile 500-ton (450-metric ton) crane, capable of lifting 100 tons (90 metric tons) at 30 feet (9 meters) erected the beams. The structure was assembled vertically, one bay at a time. A pair of knobs welded onto each column marked every floor level. Attaching the geberettes became a simple matter of slipping them over the columns and rotating them 90° at the proper floor to lock them into place; this accounts for their somewhat unusual shape. Then the trusses were pinned between the geberettes, which in turn were tied together. A full bay took 10 days to assemble. The entire erection process was simple, speedy, and virtually problem-free, requiring only eight months to complete. And that included pouring the concrete floors.

The Development of the Servicing

Like the structure, the servicing is governed by the same principles of growth and change which led to the visual expression of the way the building works. The greatest portion of the visual stimuli is provided by the blue double-duct, variable-volume, all-air and all-electric air-handling units that comprise the Rue du Renard elevation. There are 13 units, one for each bay. In keeping with the standard French color codes to denote air-handling units, they are painted blue. (Likewise water and electricity are colored green and yellow.) The variable-volume system was picked to allow specific areas to be closed down or independently controlled, in addition to catering to flexible and variable lighting installations, while also allowing for future boxes/offices to be installed and linked into the main systems. An all-air unit was chosen to avoid distribution of water in spaces containing works of art and books. And an all-electric building turned out to be both more economical and less polluting than the alternatives.

In a fully serviced artificial environment such as Beaubourg, mechanicals typically require 10 percent of the floor area of the building while consuming about 40 percent of the total budget. Half of the primary mechanical zones were concentrated below grade, from which they feed the space above; the remainder were placed on the

Opposite page: The geberette is slipped onto the knobbed column and rotated a quarter turn to lock it into place. The knob on the column becomes the attachment point for the cross-bracing of the facade and the support for the passerelles.

Above: The trussed beams supporting the floors are hooked into the geberette to balance the weight of the cantilever while the geberettes are joined at their outer ends by vertical ties. The structure was created vertically, one bay at a time.

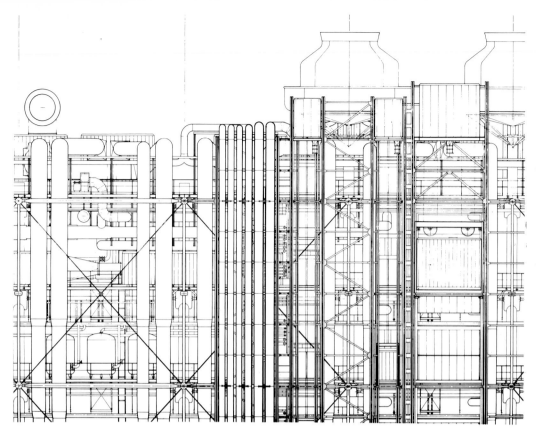

roof, feeding vertically down outside on the Rue du Renard facade. All crossovers between, say, electrical conduits and sprinklers, occur on the exterior; once the services penetrate the curtain wall, they run neatly between the structural beams, an arrangement providing both maximum headroom and visual clarity.

The decision to expose the mechanicals led to new problems related to the training of architects, engineers, and contractors. The appearance of services have traditionally been deemed to be of so little importance that one finds them simply indicated on working drawings by dimensionless single lines. In a random order each service subcontractor supplies and fixes his own supports, attaching them to whatever happens to be the nearest piece of building fabric in whatever fashion strikes his fancy. And, of course, hidden behind suspended ceilings lies the result of the tradesmen's free-for-all, an inarticulate spaghetti of tubing and joinery. As there is not any precedent for displaying the mechanical servicing in a building of this size, it was necessary to indulge in as lengthy as possible a period of mutual enlightenment, while bearing in mind the fact that time was short and cost control imperative.

This was compounded by our commitment for quality and maintenance control by having all mechanical elements arrive on the site prefabri-cated and prefinished. That meant that while every floor and every bay may look identical to the casual observer, they actually are not. Fully half of them vary in either the detailed realization of the facade or the servicing plan, requiring individual consideration of each bay. To provide future flexibility, we were forced to develop the prototypical plan and section for the worst of all possible cases, namely, when the suspension system for hanging the ductwork would be the most skewed. To answer to changing needs, one must initially allow some diversity in the design so that in the future elements such as mezzanines or bathrooms might be added or subtracted. For example, the building is fitted throughout with waste collection boxes in the floor sandwich capable of being quickly hooked up to movable toilet capsules with fireman-type connectors. The bathrooms that were finally built are more permanent than the ideal, although additional toilets have already been added to accommodate the vast number of visitors. The same goes for the grid of water and power lines threaded beneath the piazza which are used for such events as the circus, the children's tent, and the flower stalls.

By treating services as an erector set of exposed components, we were able to speed up the erection and cut down on some of the maintenance required, which counteracted some of the

headaches we endured. Mechanical subcontractors, professionals not exactly known for their love of innovation or commitment to the ideal of future flexibility, were more than reluctant to be responsible for the supply and fixing of supports onto which they had little or no services to attach. Nor for that matter did they delight in inventing new support systems with higher fire ratings than those currently in existence. But these agonies pale beside the greater dilemma of fire protection.

Fire Protection

Probably the major flaw in the scheme lay in our inability to develop a new technique of fireproofing structural steel. Here we had a major building totally constructed out of steel and backed by considerable political muscle, once-in-a-lifetime conditions for which a steel manufacturer could research and solve this problem. We actually believed that we would make a major breakthrough and find a system of making the steel itself incombustible without resorting to the considerable expenditure of creative effort required in the search for elegant ways to ad hoc fireproofing. It didn't happen.

This left us very much at the mercy of the local fire codes. Or rather the Parisian fire department.

As this was the first public building of *grand hauteur*, every regulation ever promulgated in the city of Paris since antiquity was applied in the most stringent manner conceivable to the tune of 50 million francs, some 10 percent of the total construction budget. While no architect in his right mind would ever want to deliberately construct a building in which people could perish of fire (or for that matter, anything else), regulations might have been a bit more imaginatively handled.

Since the fire brigade's ladders could not stretch beyond 90 feet (28 meters), the top floor could be no higher. That meant it had to shrink 64 feet (19 meters), virtually eliminating all the open space within the open structural cage, as we squeezed the program bulk into a smaller volume. Where our floor areas surpassed the regulation maximum fire compartment size of nearly 100,000 cubic feet (2,800 cubic meters), they had to be subdivided to make them smaller. In general normal dynamic fire protection systems where a fuse is broken releasing a steel shutter were forbidden save in small quantities; it led to the arbitrary chopping of the museum floor into two halves, which compromised the tenet of absolute flexibility and transparency (although both halves can easily be reunited later). No inflammable materials (except for the art and the books) were

allowed anywhere within the building shell. These included wood, plastics, fabrics, composite materials, and even padding on chairs, leaving steel, concrete, and asbestos as the only materials we could use.

Design was governed by the fairly straightforward principle of "separate and extinguish." It affected the visual appearance of virtually every element. The trussed beams, for example, appear structurally overweight simply because the structural steel is wrapped in a blanket of fibrous material and then encased in a stainless steel armor to prevent it from melting in a two-hour fire. The building is, of course, sprinklered throughout with either water or halogen gas (used to protect areas with a lot of electricity running through them and to keep from ruining the books and artworks by flooding). In addition there is an elaborate mechanical smoke exhaust system controlled by a computerized rise-of-temperature detection system. Furthermore, a special series of back-up dampers in the ducting prevent smoke from being blown through the rest of the building.

The fireproofing system gets considerably less clear-cut outside the enclosing wall zone. While the exterior steelwork is left exposed, depending on distance, screening, and sprinklers to keep it from failing in the event of fire, the elevation plane itself was by far the trickiest to design. Its various fire systems range from the exterior panels themselves to water-filled columns. The hollow columns are very thick at the bottom and very thin at the top, requiring a pump to make sure that the water circulates completely through them.

Every infill panel in the curtain wall marks a stage in the hierarchy of protection, progressing step by step from the wired glazing to the clear double glazing to the solid panels to those sprinklered panels which actually touch the geberettes themselves. Added to this is a collection of roll-down steel shuttering to protect the glass, which manages also to provide both manual and automatic sun control.

Even more complicated is the Rue du Renard elevation. In addition to being fully sprinklered, all mechanical support elements have half-, two- or three-hour fire ratings, depending on the service they support. Precautions are also taken to avoid half-hour services collapsing onto two-hour

services should a fire occur. With the help of the fire department, the infill in the curtain wall has evolved from completely transparent to totally solid. It necessitated replanning most of the interiors three full years after work had begun.

It is impossible to divorce the building from its legal, technical, political, and economic context. At the same time, a major part of any design approach is the way constraints may be absorbed and wherever possible inverted into positive elements. On one hand, new technical needs and regulations, political dictums, and changing user requirements make it difficult to control the building; on the other hand, the way that the building overcame these constraints is a measure of the success or failure of both the building and its philosophy.

Every day over 25,000 people visit the Centre, as many as visit the Louvre and the Eiffel Tower put together, which is 20,000 more visitors than the building was programmed for. This has naturally taxed some of the facilities. To minimize the crush on the escalators, another run needs to be clipped on. This is quite easy as the escalators are hung in a steel cradle which is screwed into the end of the geberettes; those not supporting escalators have their ends capped.

Other things have changed over time. Functions have shifted. Cinemas have been added, a change that proved fairly simple to accommodate despite high smoke exhaust requirements necessary in theaters. More toilet capsules have been added. The number of entrances has dwindled from the original thirteen doors with the possibility of placing doors wherever needed to only two entries, leading to long lines. The administration offices may move out into an adjoining building as the permanent staff has more than doubled since the inception.

The street-oriented Parisian public has taken over every space given to it, starting with the neighboring street shops and piazza and continuing through the public spaces in the building, and are now even conquering the departments in the Centre. These are only the first of many changes as Beaubourg accommodates itself to the needs of the people, envisioned or not. This is what we mean when we call it an architecture of possibilities.

HARRY SEIDLER

Born in Vienna in 1923, Harry Seidler attended the University of Manitoba, where he earned a Bachelor of Architecture in 1944. From there he won a scholarship to do graduate work at Harvard University, which was just coming into flower under Walter Gropius. After receiving his Master of Architecture, he spent a year with Josef Albers at Black Mountain College in North Carolina. Returning to New York, he worked for Marcel Breuer for several years and then briefly for Oscar Niemeyer in Brazil before emigrating to Australia to open his own firm.

Like most architects, his practice first consisted exclusively of private houses, which are most notable for their elegant structural expression. Unquestionably the best of these is his own split-level home built into a spectacular hillside site. Particularly innovative is his use of several upturned concrete channels that rightside up form the floors and upside down form the roof structure and sun protection. From the early houses he graduated to multifamily housing, characterized by increasingly sophisticated split-level plans, as well as to larger buildings. One of the most spectacular is the Australia Square circular office tower, a 50-story concrete structure engineered like much of Seidler's work by Pier Luigi Nervi. This particular building uses a single floor beam throughout, which is only possible in a circular tower and floor system. While the radial beams were poured, the precast exterior casings of the columns, which change shape as their load changes, were filled with concrete, which speeded up the construction process. This kind of integral marriage between structure and construction is typical of Seidler's work. Typical also is the sophistication of his precast concrete construction and his bold reaffirmation of the tenets of modern architecture, which is a currently unfashionable stance. His work does, however, deal with the fact that architecture is about construction, which post-Modernism, at least as it has been presented to date, has yet to seriously broach.

Seidler has won many awards for his buildings. Chief among them is the Gold Medal from the Royal Australian Institute of Architects. He has also taught at Harvard and the University of Virginia, lectured extensively, and recently published a monograph, New Settlement Strategy and Current Architectural Practice in Australia.

Support detail of the chancellery entrance of the Australian Embassy in Paris.

A side from convictions on the inevitable aesthetic aims in our time—brought into the consciousness of the designer by the systematic study of and experimentation in visual phenomena—convictions about the clear social aims to be achieved in the built environment must be allied with equally clear attitudes about the need to push forward the frontiers of technology as an integral part of all architectural thought. It is the lack of that aspect of the design process which is responsible for so much failure in modern architecture as a convincing, worthy product of our time. By contrast architecture should be expected to embody assurances not only of physical but also of aesthetic longevity.

While Western society, in spite of its desperate physical building needs and shortcomings, can still occasionally support willful, capricious, and wasteful buildings, these are becoming increasingly recognized as irrelevant and, by implication, asocial and amoral pursuits. What could possibly remain valid in building highly labor intensive, almost medievally hand-wrought structures produced at outrageously high quantity and expenditure in material that upon completion demand perpetually operating, vast energy-consuming devices to keep them barely fit for human use?

More and more they are being recognized as a hollow victory indeed, efforts leading toward a dead end in a world hungry for universally applicable devices to cope with the failing man-made environment. Even if there are still ample Texas millionaires and other instrumentalities of much wealth bent on self-aggrandisement, the once great appetite for the occasionally brilliant, purely visual results of their commissions is rapidly cloying. It is the questioning of their relevance today that by implication makes them in fact become ugly.

Above all, there must be an awareness of the realities of the day and the inevitable way these are pointing to the future. In the West in the next century, there will be no armies of unskilled labor to perform the tasks now taken for granted as an inherent aspect of architectural design. In locations such as India or Mexico it may remain valid for longer to demand high labor intensity, but in Europe, America, Canada, Australia, and other developed areas, this is already highly questionable, and its products are increasingly rejected.

Design concept and constructional means must be an integral, married part of each other. If they are divorced, lead separate lives, or point in different directions, they become invalid and are supportable only by artificial means.

The scale of the work is a major pace-setter in the design and construction relationship. Whereas it may be entirely reasonable in a small, one-of-a-kind structure to expect a substantial amount of hand labor to be expended, the ratio in a large structure must be on an entirely different basis. The balance between labor intensity and plausibility of a high-technology concept is one of scale.

Much modern architecture and some of today's most celebrated is utterly deceitful in this respect—and much of it is an outright lie. It pretends to be born of and based on a system which in truth is nothing but a tortuous procedure requiring vast amounts of medieval-style hand labor to bring it into existence. Tasks requiring acrobatic feats performed by literally armies of laborers on scaffolds are, when completed, clothed in an envelope that pretends to be stamped out by machine, utterly belying the fact of its great handmade confusion inside.

Let us think simply and realistically of the tasks.

The cardinal imperative for the designer is to find solutions which in addition to all *architectural* considerations can be produced *naturally* in a given socioeconomic climate.

In countries with high labor costs this will increasingly eliminate on-site labor, especially if it is dirty and must be performed on scaffolds.

It will eliminate structures that must be made fireproof by labor-intensive tasks.

It will force architects to devise and maximize systems of mechanization appropriate to and in tune with the particular task. These must not only include considerations of structure and cladding (as is so often the limit of prevailing thought), but encompass simultaneously integral solutions to the problems posed by all services (without the usual nightmarish afterthoughts that complicate most modern buildings).

It will make them pursue with purity and directness the problems of connections and detail which reoccur wherever identical situations generate them (in contrast with ad hoc traditional detailing which contributes so much to the high cost of building).

Architects must strive towards the exquisite understatement inherent in integrated systems which reinforce each other to take the place of today's fashionable devotion to ostentatious complexity.

Systematic solutions and their components, however, should invite variation. The more parts of a system are assembled, the more interesting and visually enticing the totality should become, rather than duller and more soul destroying as is the present-day norm.

In the shaping of elements, free reign must be

The single 800-foot (240-meter) Mutual Life and Citizens Tower occupies only 20 percent of its site. The octagonal shape resulted from the need to avoid the railway tunnels which traverse the site.

given to the expression of the laws of nature—not what is imagined to be so by many structurally naive architects, but the unassailable physical truth of statics. Great richness of expression can result from such a search, which will have that irreplaceable quality of longevity—of remaining valid—being born of the immutable and irrevocable truth of nature.

In the three buildings that will be discussed in detail here, I have attempted to recall some of the high principles and clear moral consequentiality in the work of the great formgivers who demanded a basic integrity and an intrinsic honesty of approach. Considerations of aesthetics, social use, and technology are happily married. In each, the concrete construction is systematized; it takes the best advantage of the available labor and skills; it expresses the flow of structural forces; and it is attractive enough not to need to be pasted over with finishes.

Mutual Life and Citizens Tower

To create as large a landscaped public plaza as possible, all the programmed office space in the Mutual Life and Citizens Tower in Sidney was put into a single octagonally shaped tower. The structure of the 68-story concrete building would have been conventionally solved as a "tube in tube," but this solution with its attendant closely spaced perimeter columns was considered inappropriate here because of its lack of lateral stability. Instead, only eight heavily loaded exterior columns were chosen to give maximum stiffness. The structure that finally evolved was based on a concept called the "progressive strength" concrete system.

That system of construction consists of welded self-supporting, open-web reinforcing bars for primary and secondary beams strong enough to support removable plastic form trays for pouring concrete progressively as the tower rises. First, the main beams are poured; then, the secondary ones; and finally, the slab, which is several floors below the progress of the main beams and slip-formed core above.

The system is based on the fact that the reinforcement in a beam can be adapted to provide the initial support needed to start the cycle by prefabricating it in a truss form. As the concrete develops strength, the function of the trusses changes progressively from a means of supporting the concrete to a means of reinforcing it. In this manner, the floors of the tallest concrete building in the world (808 feet, or 242.4 meters) were

erected without formwork at the rate of one completed floor (facade and all) every four days.

The long span facade beams and columns are fabricated of precast facing units simultaneously with the floors. The 6-foot (1.8-meter) deep spandrel beams alternately span 35 feet (11 meters) and 60 feet (18 meters) around the perimeter; their I-shape resulted from a desire to recess the windows for protection from the sun. The twisted shape of the exterior columns expresses the cantilever action of all tall towers, with the greatest moment-of-inertia resistance at the base where the columns are turned outward and are flush with the building form at the top where no moment occurs. Near the base of the tower the columns are tied together and to the core by curved beams which are exposed in the main entrance. Both the columns and the spandrels are constructed of precast concrete panels as the formwork into which concrete is poured.

This structural system has many advantages. Not only does it make use of the inherent load-bearing capacity of the forms, but it takes advantage of the progressive gain in strength characteristic of concrete. Its highly industrialized nature transfers the bulk of the work to the factory where there is high quality control and virtually no jointing or tolerance problems. This halves the amount

of on-site labor and more efficiently uses the remaining manpower, since the cycle for production of a story is spread over several levels. It also shortens the erection process by more than two days per floor, a five-month saving over the entire building.

A Mixed-Use Building: Australian Embassy

The program for the Australian Embassy in Paris was split into two quadrant-shaped structures: an office building with precast facade and floors and an apartment building with precast facade and Predalle floors (this system was developed in France and will be discussed below). A combination of factory and on-site prefabrication was developed. Long, identical, tapered T-beams forming the office quadrant were supported by precast, quartz-faced, structural window units and a core built by a rising-form system. Great speed of erection resulted. The precast structural facade was interrupted at the two-story high entrance and carried by a treelike, poured-in-place support which was shaped to reflect its structural effort: to bring down the loads of the curved facade and resolve them (with straight boarded formwork)

The Australian Embassy in Paris is split into two quadrant-shaped structures, one containing an office building and the other housing.

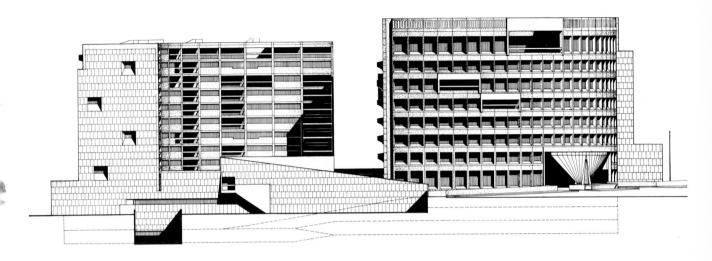

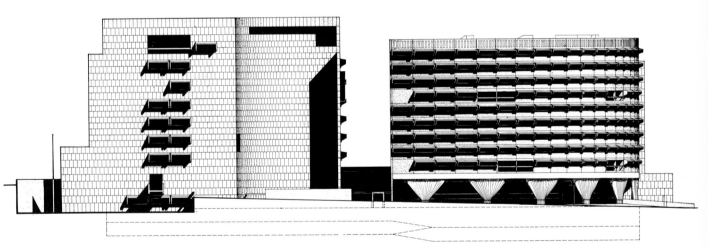

Elevations of the embassy.

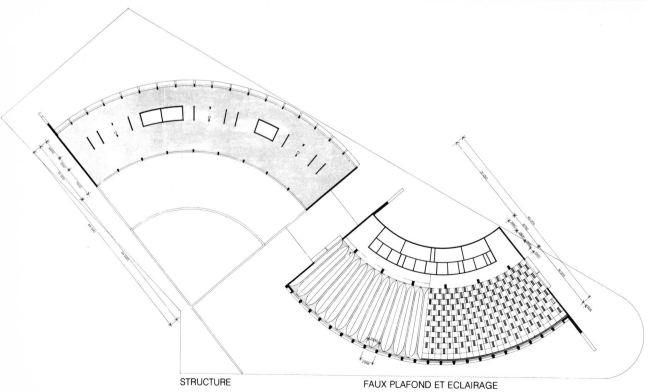

STRUCTURE   FAUX PLAFOND ET ECLAIRAGE

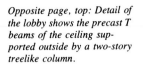

Opposite page, top: Detail of the lobby shows the precast T beams of the ceiling supported outside by a two-story treelike column.

Opposite page, bottom: Reflected ceiling plans of the Australian Embassy show the predalle structure of the apartment building and the T beams of the office block with and without the lighting.

Top, left: A crane is equipped with a special hook system for lifting the 500-square-foot (47-square-meter) panels.

Top, right: The crane is then hooked to the reinforcing trusses.

Bottom, left: The slab is picked up.

Bottom, right: The slab is then moved into place and attached. After this the balance of the slab is poured in place.

into two columns turned at right angles to the facade to give lateral stability. P.L. Nervi served as the consultant.

The apartment building was constructed from a partial system of site prefabrication of its segmental floors. The Predalle system consists of precasting the lower part of the flat slab floors on a steel platform at ground level. The upper surface is left very rough, and the concrete is steam-cured overnight. These panels, up to 500 square feet (47 square meters) in area, are then picked up by a crane and deposited on minimal formwork supported by precast facade and interior columns. The balance of the slab is then poured in place, leaving a smooth, paintable surface below, which eliminated the need for plastering. All conventional, labor-intensive concrete formwork was thus avoided.

Trade Group Offices

The program for the Trade Group Offices in Canberra included the accommodation of three interrelated federal government departments for a total office population of 3,250. Through the design we aimed to achieve an architecture of strength, simplicity, and considering its location adjacent to Australia's Seat of Federal Government, an appropriate level of formality. Any suggestion of short-lived capriciousness and fashionable intricately molded facades and sections was avoided in favor of a simple, strong silhouette. In fact, every hope of aesthetic longevity was projected. The program itself, requiring completely flexible office space, suggested a systematized approach, expressed mainly by the long-span, structural design and the implied means of construction.

The solution adopted consisted of a system of connected wings joined by vertical access cores and creating open courtyards between them. This met the aims of flexibility. Office areas for various departments are spanned from the cores in two directions; they meet, but connect only in cases where communication is required. Each half-wing is served from a core, which cuts down on complete through corridors. Other than providing the specified total occupiable floor space, there is no initial need to define the boundaries of each department.

The configuration of the scheme lent itself to a systematized structural solution which consisted of post-tensioned, precast, mass-produced concrete elements. Only one floor element, one exterior wall, and one column element needed to be produced—a basic approach which took into account the fact that the scheme had to be built in a short time.

The 50-foot (15-meter) wide, column-free wings were spanned by identical prestressed T-beam planks, 4 feet 9½ inches (146.1 centimeters) wide. The prefabricated floor planks organi-

Opposite page: A typical facade of the Trade Group Offices shows the long-span precast facade girders acting as bris soleil. The knobs visible on the beams support the precast T beams spanning the depth of the office space inside.

Below: Key:

1. Spandrel I beam
2. Modular floor plank T beam
3. Window cleaning safety track
4. Curtain track
5. Heat-absorbing glass and neoprene gasket
6. Induction units
7. Secondary chilled water supply and return
8. High-pressure air supply
9. Skirting
10. Prestressing anchorage and cover
11. Prestressing tendon coupler
12. Topping and vinyl tiles
13. Prestressing tendons to I beams
14. Plenum return air
15. Inner zone air supply
16. Suspended modular ceiling
17. Recessed fluorescent light fixtures
18. Beam penetrations for services
19. Prestressing tendons to T beams
20. Cast-in-place concrete beam and slab
21. Brick infill
22. Precast concrete facing panels
23. Cast-in-place concrete column
24. Precast concrete column
25. Provisional stack
26. Duct casing

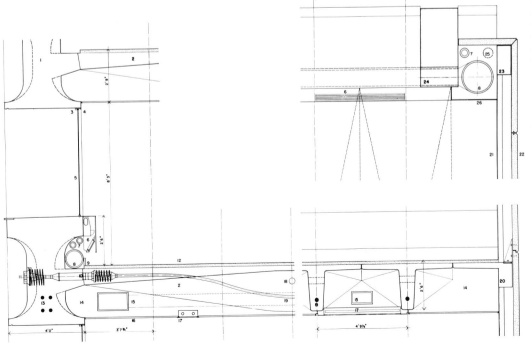

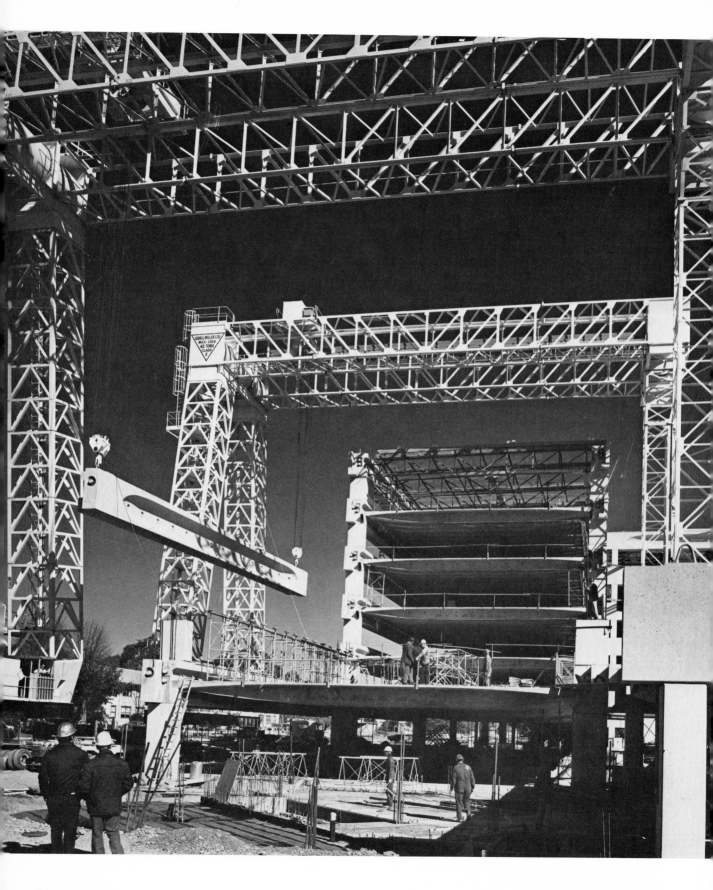

cally change form from a rectangular support to a T in the center. Two structural facts dictated this design: the T is the most efficient concrete unit for resisting deflection in a 50-foot span and the most efficient concrete unit to be supported is a slab-on-line support. Their shape allowed for the passage of longitudinal service ducts near the supports. All units were post-tensioned individually and to each other.

The program required facades with integral exterior protection from the sun. Upon examination of the most essential shading need, the outline of a sufficient profile that spans 80 feet (24 meters) was developed. The shape expressed the parabolic change from solid at the ends to resist shear to an I in the center to resist bending. They were produced on the site and lifted by moving gantries. The longitudinal exterior walls of the office wings consisted of spandrel beams, with two and three such spans respectively on the short and long sides of the courtyards and with glass between their inner edges forming the office windows.

Columns were also precast and arranged in pairs to provide structurally desirable simple supports for the spandrel beams and to facilitate exit points to the fire stairs attached to each long wing. The space between the paired columns also contained provisional plumbing stacks and condensation lines from induction units.

Not only do the profiles of both floor planks and spandrel beams follow their logical structural outlines, but they provide for the appropriate horizontal service arteries. The installation of the air conditioning consisted of a low-pressure air system serving the inner zone of office space and a high-pressure system serving the induction units under the windows.

The interior zone system requiring little flexibility was chosen because people and lighting loads are relatively constant. Not much air is needed to supply the two zones on each wing; for this, a simple all-air system was most economical.

At the perimeter, however, the situation was different. Much flexibility was needed to cater to the variation in interior loads of people and lights and the variation in the load due to the sun's changing orientation. To eliminate downdrafts from the windows in cold weather, an under-window air supply system was preferable. In addition, the savings in mechanical room space led to the choice of an induction unit system.

Flexibility was achieved by the use of separate

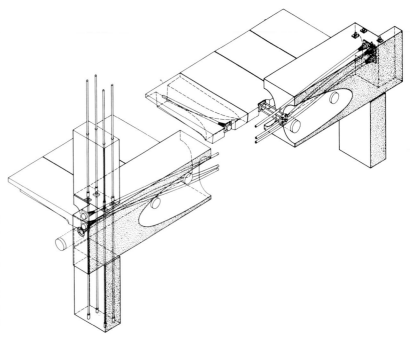

units for each basement area, which allowed economic off-hours operation of any system. This meant that the office block system could be operated independently to permit a quarter, half, or three-quarters of the building to be air conditioned at any one time.

Air is returned through a ceiling plenum. This decision reduces the quantities of supply air required to condition the space, which reduces the size of the air handling unit. It also provides efficient smoke exhaust from the office space, board rooms, and other areas of heavy smoking. It eliminates the use of door grills in partitions and improves the efficiency and life of light fixtures.

The foregoing examples constitute one designer's efforts to solve problems consequentially, following a clear methodology of approach. The fusing of structure/construction/economy with clear aesthetic aims and practical demands of building users is the essence of mainstream modern architecture's philosophy.

The countless recent buildings throughout the world based on the prevalent out-of-balance, one-sided, capricious approach are threatening to divert the inevitable direction of architectural development. The general public's understandable disenchantment with new building and the environment has been the result. By stressing the need for the integrated approach demonstrated here, we hope to stimulate a desirable reorientation.

Above: Axonometric of the precast concrete assembly showing the post-tensioning rods.

Opposite page: At the Trade Group Offices the construction of precast facade beams (each weighing 80 tons) and floor elements (each weighing 11 tons) is by means of three-legged steel gantries traveling on rails and designed to rotate at the corners.

NORMAN FOSTER

Born in Manchester in 1935, Norman Foster entered the university there and received his architectural diploma. In addition he won the Heywood Medal and a traveling fellowship, which helped him go to the United States to study at Yale. After earning a Masters of Architecture there in 1962, he returned to England and established his own firm, first in partnership with his wife and Richard and Su Rogers and later with only his wife. He has taught extensively in both Europe and America, and is a past vice-president of the Architectural Association. He also serves as an examiner and member of the Visiting Board of Education for the Royal Institute of British Architects.

While his early projects were chiefly modest contour-hugging houses, Foster's designs began to veer in the direction of large-span loose-fit umbrella buildings, assembled out of dry factory-made components, which are also low in energy use. Over time the process—of deriving the program; defining its social goals; finding the simplest, most efficient shed structure which affords the most flexibility for growth and change; and then erecting it—began to get increasingly more sophisticated. This can be seen in the progression from the Modern Art Glass Building to the Sainsbury Center. While both buildings have essentially the same sectional profile, the resolution of the exterior panel system, for instance, is far more developed in the latter building.

Foster is currently working on a highrise condominium/office tower/gallery addition to New York's Whitney Museum; a fabric-roofed, large-span structure covering a transportation interchange and urban complex for the London Transport Executive; a technical park for IBM in Middlesex; and a house for his own family in London, in which he is experimenting with glue technology borrowed from the aircraft industry.

The search for more dynamically flexible buildings, as in the Sainsbury Center, is an attempt to optimize on the constant of change.

rchitecture is a pragmatic art. There are many people involved in the building process, many possibilities inherent in the problem itself, many ways to arrange the spaces, to marry the building to its site, and techniques to construct it. Design is really a tool. It is a means of integrating and resolving the inevitable conflicts that range from public/private to socially acceptable/commercially viable in order to reconcile the artistic aspects of making a building with cost, time, and quality control. By trying to optimize all the givens within a consistent framework of values upon which design decisions are based, we hope to arrive at a whole which is more than the sum of its parts.

Tantamount among our values is a conviction that we can utilize and develop new technologies for social ends. It translates into a process of probing to determine the requirements of the users, which is both an inseparable part of the design approach and a means to question preconceptions and propose alternatives. For instance, a research project for the Spastics Society was concerned with the special problems posed by severely mentally and physically handicapped children. Research into existing buildings showed traditional toilets, despite extreme incontinency common to such children and the physical and psychological difficulties posed to the staff. In a prototype school pioneered by the Spastics Society with the Inner London Education Authority, toilets were completely reinterpreted as a glazed central area with low screens for the children's privacy, but good views for the staff onto the adjacent teaching areas and the garden court beyond. By pulling all the ventilating air through this space, there were

The structure for the Palmerston Special School for Handicapped Children pioneered by the Spastics Society provides generous spans over open-planned flexible space with minimal means.

no problems of smells or need for lobbies. (A larger scale version showing the same principle of pressurizing spaces was used in the Willis Faber Building to incorporate the restaurant and pool into a continuous three-story, two-acre volume.) At a detail level the problems of heating and lighting such buildings were quite challenging when we realized that some children could burn themselves on radiators or suffer eye damage when staring up into bright light sources without being able to summon help. The successful resolution of these and other problems enabled better utilization of teachers who were able to make more time available for the real priority: the children's therapy.

In addition to an attempt to fit the building optimally to its program, we are concerned with responding positively to the site context. Our early houses have very low profiles dug into their hillside sites to minimize their visual impact on the surroundings and merge with them; one Cornwall house is virtually buried beneath its sodded roof. In contrast the Vestby "offices in a forest" project responds to its context by lifting the building off the ground. It sits on undercarriages of steel stilts in an attempt to conserve the Norwegian forest and protect it from the usual ravages caused by the contractors' activities. Lightweight components, easily transportable through forest trails or moved by helicopter to more remote locations, can be bolted together quickly with the minimum of fuss by small teams. This approach includes concepts of low energy to drive the building. To get the most from the low sunlight, mirrors are to be used to bounce light into the heart of the building in order to burn off the waste snow that would accumulate on the building's north side. Similarly, utilization of the cold water at the bottom of the fjord is a viable alternative to high-energy air conditioning. Furthermore, paper, sewage, and water can be recycled to avoid polluting the fjord with human waste.

We have taken sympathy with the context a step further in our constant preoccupation with interior orientation—particularly natural top light and the liberating qualities of transparency. This idea was transformed in our first houses into open plan spaces, with changing levels and lots of skylights always orienting to the view outside; by the time we got around to the Willis Faber Building it became an office landscape surrounding a skylit winter garden.

We have also been interested in flexibility in buildings as a way of resolving the conflicts between public and private, the community and the individual, and short-term and long-term re-

Top: The project for Vestby "offices in a forest" attempts to minimize intrusions on the site, so the building is lifted off the forest floor.

Bottom: Elevation detail of the Reliance Controls Factory; this was the first building where we developed ideas about the integration of services, structure, and skin.

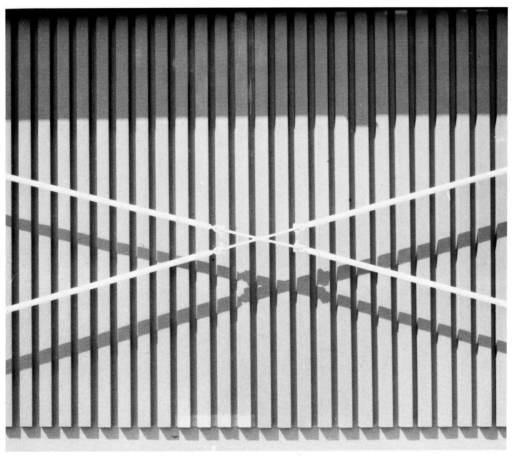

Right: This Cornwall house with its sod roof is dug into its hillside site as a way of blending it with the setting.

Below: This research project shows the potential for multilevel spaces within an umbrella enclosure. It is now being realized in built form as a technical park for IBM at Greenford near London.

quirements. Flexibility for choice, change, and growth has its problems as well as its bonuses. In the end it means resolving and integrating such conflicting requirements as servicing and structure, heating, lighting, and cooling. It led us to a series of multiuse umbrella buildings such as the Reliance Controls Factory. There a pavilion form was chosen since its inbuilt democratic implications of everybody being on the same plane as everyone else were considered more socially appropriate for a clean, rapid growth electronics industry in the 20th century than the usual workers' shed and management box, with its overtones of "we and they," "clean and dirty," "posh and scruffy," "back and front." Technically, such a form also offered a logic for dealing with limited time and money, as well as provided the potential for quick and easy changes. Whenever possible, elements had to do double or even triple duty; for example, the metal roof profile acted as a lighting reflector for recessed fluorescent tubes in addition to serving structurally as a stiff diaphragm.

Towards an Appropriate Technology

The Reliance Controls Factory marked a turning point in our attitudes toward materials. While the early houses were all built partially out of traditional materials and partially out of industrial components, we were becoming increasingly disenchanted with so-called traditional materials, their anachronisms, and the problems of quality control posed by the breakdown of craft traditions. In one early house, the Creek Vean Waterfront House built in Cornwall, we attempted to combine blockwork with structural gaskets. Quality control usually consisted of condemning areas of blockwork to be slavishly rebuilt. Even the "locally matching" blocks were a charade as they had to be freighted from Liverpool, some three hundred miles away. Trying to build this way left us in no doubt about the shortfalls and labor-intensive indulgencies involved in so-called craft trades. Which left us searching for a way of making buildings exclusively out of dry components.

We did some research into a kit-of-parts approach for educational systems that produced interior layouts which would be responsive to dynamic change within an infinite variety of plan forms. Essentially, these were highly integrated, lightweight service umbrellas, developed with a strong awareness of the performance specification design approach and integrated umbrellas of the concurrent California Schools Construction Systems Development.

Later, this approach was incorporated into a project for IBM in which a wide variety of functions were grouped under one roof, rather than the traditional collection of diverse buildings, in order to maximize flexibility and optimize the use of space. Initially, the building housed pilot main office functions such as computers, offices, amenities, and a communications center, but has since been in a constant state of flux. Since the program was never fixed, things are still being moved around eight years later; the canteen has changed its location several times, the entrances have been shifted three. The schedule was so tight (less than a year for design and build) that IBM assumed that an "off-the-shelf" timber building would be the only answer. The budget had been set accordingly at around half the price of a tradi-

The pilot main office for IBM unites all the separate functions into one umbrella, similar in spirit to the Reliance Factory.

tional permanent building. IBM had about half of its British operation in such temporary structures and the remainder in permanent buildings (its statistics are similar to those of the Los Angeles school system), which tells a great deal about the constant of change. Within such constraints, the only solution was an integration of essential dry systems, which could be likened to an erector set. Ironically, this has produced a permanent building, as now defined by the owners' and city building authority's terms of reference.

Perhaps our most minimal exercise in serviced space was the air-supported office for Computer Technology. The structure was environmentally engineered to enable 80 people to work throughout the year in conditions more comfortable than the standard factory shed to which it was attached. This was the first application of an ultrathin membrane enclosure for sedentary activities. The erection time was under an hour, and the kit-of-parts approach enabled interior systems to be installed in less than a week. The structure was eventually removed to provide a parking lot for a new multiuse permanent building, which utilized gasketed

aluminum and foam sandwich panels derived from the automotive and insulated container industries. This and the later Modern Art Glass project with its wrap-around cladding were related to component developments for the Sainsbury Center.

With the kit-of-parts approach, the building becomes an integration of systems rooted in social and technical research. In its traditional sense, this includes the structural, mechanical, and electrical. In its broadest it includes the filigree of interior systems involved with the flux and change of movement and activities. The links between research and practice are close and aided by continuous model studies at varying scales, from full size mockups of rooms to testing programs for prototypical components.

In 1968 Buckminster Fuller approached us to collaborate with him on his first English project, the Samuel Beckett Theater, which eventually took the form of what could be best described as a submarine under an Oxford quadrangle. This collaboration expanded into a wider partnership which continues to pose radical alternatives to

Top: The erection of the bubble of this air-supported structure for Computer Technology took about an hour and the entire construction sequence a few weeks.

Bottom: This pneumatic structure, later resold, provided virtually rent-free accommodation for a year.

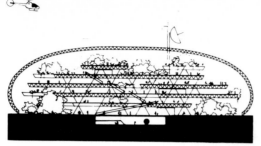

conventional built form. For example, the Clima-
troffice project was projected at the time of the
Willis Faber scheme and shows the potential for
grouping a mix of existing buildings and new
activities under an all-embracing structural skin to
create a total microclimate.

Both the Willis Faber and the Sainsbury Center
are interesting as recent examples of our design
philosophy and as culminations of the last 15
years of work. Both are made completely out of
industrial components. Both are umbrella structures taken beyond the ordinary factory-plus-
office combination in a way that maximizes the
social amenities and the standards offered to the
people who have to use the building. More than
anything else, technology is only a means. While
in no way underestimating the importance of such
means, they are, after all, means and not ends in
themselves. The ends are social, generated by
people rather than building hardware.

Willis Faber + Dumas

Willis Faber + Dumas, a large international firm
of insurance brokers whose coverage has run the
gamut from the Titanic to the NASA moon buggy,
wanted a typical office, a paper factory. The challenge was to produce something better than the
kind of Dickensian squalor in which they seemed
to exist. In a fundamental sense, the building is
really about the concept of people and their workplace. Our preoccupation with standards in industry and commerce was rooted as much in research
into the work process as in an interest in social
change and a sensitivity to the proportion of time
spent in the workplace. We placed an emphasis on
raising standards and providing amenities to at-
tract the most talented, competent people and to
keep them happy enough with their working conditions so that they would be highly productive in
their jobs. Consequently, the two office floors
were sandwiched between a host of amenity
facilities: swimming pool and coffee bar, gymnasium and restaurant. The roof is virtually a glass
restaurant pavilion set in a landscaped garden. All

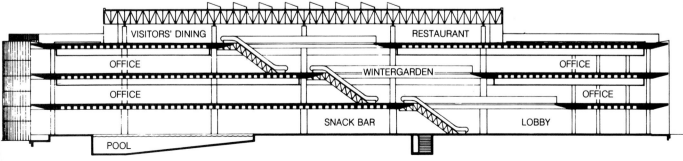

VISITORS' DINING   RESTAURANT

OFFICE   WINTERGARDEN   OFFICE

OFFICE   OFFICE

SNACK BAR   LOBBY

POOL

At Willis Faber all floors are connected and penetrated by a vertical movement space. This center of gravity in the building is important both functionally and symbolically.

floors are connected and penetrated by a vertical space containing banks of escalators, palm trees, and daylight from generously glazed skylights. The proportion of amenity area to work area is high, especially if the near acre of roof garden is included in the equation.

Emphasis on the workplace and related standards is best expressed by a virtual about-face from the traditional office building. There, typically, standards are highest for the visitor and gradually lowered until you reach the user—for example, entrance lobby areas have finishes and fittings that gobble up the top slice of the funds and reflect a total disparity with the working floors.

The reverse is true at Willis Faber. The entrance is an exposed concrete structure (enlivened with emulsion paint), studded rubber (the same as in the boiler room and lavatories), and demountable metal partitions (like everywhere else). This compares with carpet, custom-designed ceilings, and glare-free light fixtures throughout the two office floors. There is no question of a reaction against fine finishes; it's merely how you define priorities and reflect them in the allocation of fixed resources (i.e., money). Usually, the workspace is "out of sight and out of mind," bypassed by the grim anonymity of elevator cars and the drab monotony of corridors—orientation is the elevator floor, the button you push, the number on the door. Here the reverse is everywhere apparent. Movement is open, literally in the sun, and social contact is natural and relaxed across the spectrum of the company. Orientation is immediate; you always know where you are. The barriers are few and seldom visual.

Management, establishing an "open door" approach in their original quarters, is here reflected by a virtual absence of doors. The planned cellular office for the deputy chairman was lost en route in the design process, and the "Directors' Dining Room" became a piece of furniture design to separate a part of the main restaurant. Even that has now become a visitors' dining room. The kind of spaces described are in no manner fixed for the future. Indeed, the acoustic and lighting technology which enables them to work at present also provides the flexibility for them to be adapted to quite different patterns.

The plan form and cross section are a response to the need to weave a large new building into the edge fabric of an historic town. The key factor was to adopt a very low, deep building, which enabled us to equate an economically feasible content with a low profile. There were other spinoffs as well: fewer larger floors provided more efficient space utilization, greater flexibil-

ity, and far lower energy consumption. Further, by pushing the building to the limit of the site boundaries, the original street pattern was reinforced.

The building is the outcome of a team approach in which the key was to shift the traditional roles of those concerned with designing and fabrication. For example, many activities were streamed in parallel during the early stages of the project. Research into the program and the inner workings of the company proceeded concurrently with studies into energy optimization, preliminary planning, and construction possibilities. This was essential on a crash program: two years of feverish design and building activity with a minimum construction period. During the complexities of demolitions and utilities diversions, the architects were more involved as management consultants than as practitioners of any normal design-based skill. A briefing guide was specifically developed to provide insight into the client's organization. In collaboration with the client, a joint management structure was established, which was in direct communication with the board at regular intervals and briefed other consultants as necessary.

Collaboration began so early that it actually preceded the definition and purchase of the site itself. The acquisition pattern proved to be one of the most difficult things to come to grips with. We would be given a site and we would be designing away for it while there would be negotiations for another parcel of land across the street. We would receive a phone call saying that it was almost purchased and could we do a scheme to show how the building would be if we had that part as well, which meant closing the road. So we would do a scheme for that, which would no sooner be finished than the client would be negotiating on the other side of the site altogether and we would be designing for that. We had scheme on scheme on scheme, which lasted a few months until it became apparent that the real estate process was so volatile that it was impossible to reflex quickly enough with traditional one-of-a-kind design responses. Careful analysis of the work study which generated the built form, as well as the ground conditions under the building (which included a high water table and all the continental telephone cable from that part of the country), together with insight into the process of site acquisition, provided the main clues. A uniform 44-foot (13.5-meter) square column grid provided an acceptable cost threshold, related well to office planning constraints, and could straddle such fixed elements as the swimming pool, roads, and loading docks. (In a building which has no front or back, the docks have to be brought inside to respect

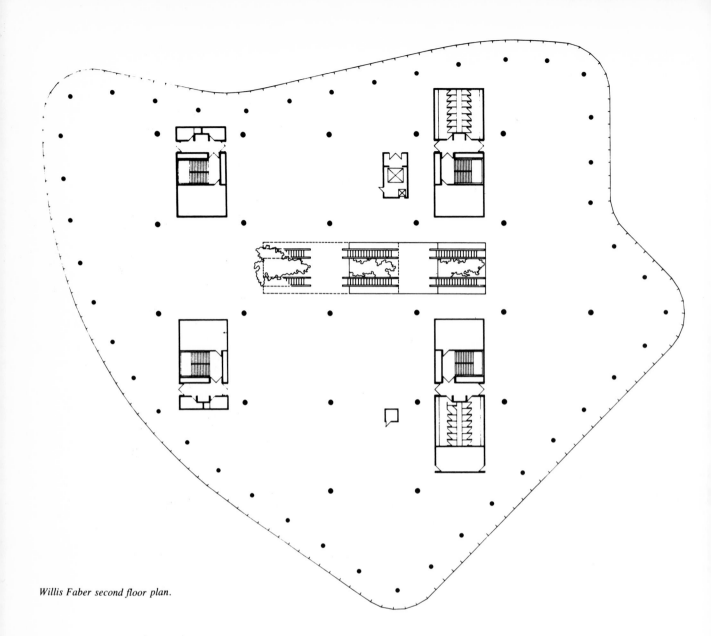

Willis Faber second floor plan.

good street manners.) Furthermore, an edge necklace of columns tuned the perimeter to closely follow the lines of existing street boundaries. Once we had the system, the client could play real estate games to his heart's content and even buy up all of Ipswich. It didn't matter.

In addition to anticipating the mechanics of building swiftly and economically on a very tight urban site, the detail development of the structure was strongly influenced by the constraints of the servicing systems. The waffle slab eliminated downturned beams throughout and provided a structure handsome enough to stand in its own right—good for the budget (no need to paste over it) and good for the schedule (fewer trades). In its final form the structure was boiled down to remarkably few elements: a set of interior columns and slab, another set of edge columns, and a cantilever strip.

The structure was the only site-based wet trade. Everything else was shop fabricated for quality control, cost, speed of erection, a belief and delight in the materials of the age, and economy of means. This also meant a shift in roles; if the product was not available ready made (and hardly anything was, in the integrated sense of the word), then we designed one and collaborated with manufacturers to produce it. This meant encouragement to industry where appropriate and frequent use of full-scale tests and mockups. A summary of the history of the glazed facade provides insight into the relationship of the design and the management techniques, which, in our view, made creative aims technically feasible.

The suspended glass wall was a response to the notion that most people are happier being able to see the outside, provided they do not suffer some discomfort as a consequence. In a deep building the effect of large glazed perimeters defining circulation routes is relatively insignificant on energy loads (unlike shallow plans where it makes quite a drastic difference). Also, in deep buildings the proportion of glass has to be generous to ensure that everybody, and not just those sitting closest to the windows, has contact with the exterior. This led to the consideration of several alternate systems that would combine such qualities as transparency with acoustic and solar control. An awareness that glass is at its strongest in tension prompted the concept of a curtain suspended from the top edge of the building. Unfortunately we were unable to convince anyone outside the office that it was technically feasible. For this reason all the interior perspectives of that period show a steel mullion system designed for the project and tested out on a smaller installation in Thamesmead. Eventually, enough calculations

and technical details emerged to convince the manufacturers that the idea was not only viable but very attractive on a cost basis, which was hardly surprising since it reduced elements to just glass and glue.

We were more than happy to trade our design know-how for design warranties backed by the manufacturers. This seemed more appropriate to our role as architects attempting a progression of ideas rather than getting locked into the marketing of one specific system. We had always viewed the design process as a vehicle for generating systems that were usable beyond an immediate one-of-a-kind solution. That is why we have put so much effort into researching integrated umbrella systems and kits-of-parts. As for the suspended glass wall, the manufacturers now market it as a freely available system. Through a similar process the studded green flooring, lighting, and escalators have also found their way into the catalogs and trade literature of their manufacturers.

The office floor and ceiling systems had a similar development, attempted in the spirit of integrating normally separate systems. For example, the parabolic light fittings were designed to link with the ceiling and also provide the air supply and return for office areas as well as sprinkler runs and a separate emergency lighting system. This compares with the more usual proliferation and redundancy in separate suspended elements brought together in a kind of on-site shotgun marriage. Likewise the electrical power and telephone lines on the office floors telegraph through the lighting grid above and below. Aware that flexibility is always thwarted by fixed trunking runs and that wet screeds take forever (like plastering, the bottom seems to have dropped out of that particular trade), we searched for viable alternatives. The result is a platform floor system (which is conceptually similar to a suspended ceiling) developed by manufacturers for this project, with continuous lines of easily removable access panels. The goals were speed, cost, appearance, and maximum flexibility in random order; it would be extremely difficult to define a hierarchy at that time or in retrospect.

The design development and final definition of facilities and standards were inextricably linked with continuous financial appraisals—quite the opposite of a static program and cost response. A wide variety of options were examined and always related back to a basic yardstick of minimum shell cost. Alternatives were evaluated with particular sensitivity to cost-in-use. The exterior, for example, is virtually maintenance-free: the glass wall almost wipes its own face, and apart from an occasional haircut, the turf roof looks after itself.

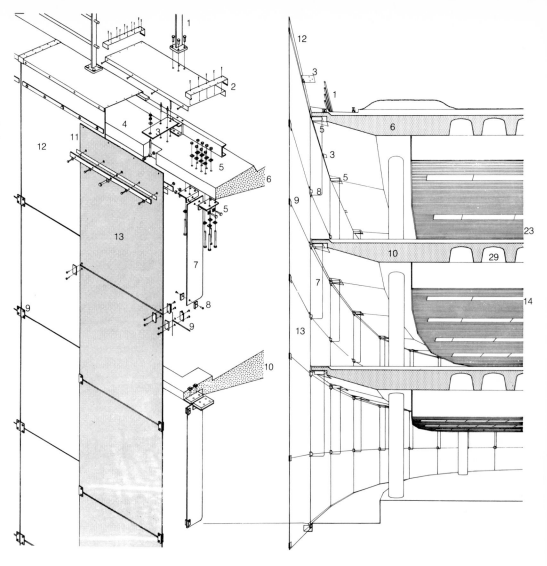

Right: Exploded drawing shows typical Willis Faber glass wall assembly details.

Far right: Wall section.

Opposite page, top: Section perspective through the floor-ceiling sandwich.

Opposite page, bottom: Typical Willis Faber office space.

Key:

1. Aluminum handrail support
2. Top flashing: folded aluminum sheet
3. Suspension bolt supporting plate
4. Suspension bolt
5. Roof supports for fins bolted through slabs
6. Roof slab
7. Reinforced clear glass fin
8. Patch fitting fin component restrains horizontal movement only
9. Patch fitting plate component split vertically to allow differential movement between facets
10. Typical floor slab
11. Fiber gasket
12. Top clamping strip bolted through glass
13. Tempered bronze-tinted glass
14. Fluorescent light fixture

15. Air diffuser
16. Main supply air duct
17. Flexible air duct connector
18. Air return plenum
19. Lighting cable track
20. Integrated ceiling and light fixture support
21. Sprinkler pipe
22. Sprinkler head
23. Aluminum ceiling channels (acoustic mat above)
24. Platform floor
25. Telephone distribution box
26. Electrical supply track
27. Socket outlet connector
28. Electrical and telephone access panels in carpet
29. Concrete waffle slab

Considerable ingenuity was deployed to minimize the cost of potential fringe benefits and thereby encouraged their introduction. For instance, a landscaped roof is certainly more expensive than asphalt. However, because we made it stronger than we needed, it acted as such a good insulating quilt that the traditional expansion joint across the entire building, with its attendant double rows of columns and piles, was eliminated. This led to increased energy savings. Similarly, we decided to expose the innards of the escalators so that you could see the whole thing working. In the same spirit and as a reaction to an innate dislike of swimming in a washbasin with a rim, we designed a swimming pool where the water level is flush with the surrounding floor. Then there was the problem of what to put in the show window of the insurance company: we decided on a display of all the mechanical equipment.

For financial justification the building had to have sublet potential. The change could be straightforward: the wintergarden could function as a semipublic space used by all office tenants; each floor has four cores enclosing escape stairs and utilities allowing up to four major subdivisions accessed from the interior court; and the mechanical systems allow total subdivision into cellular offices if required.

The Sainsbury Center for the Visual Arts

The first meeting with Sir Robert and Lady Sainsbury left no doubt about their attitudes to art galleries. They had an obvious distaste for monuments, a belief that works of art should be enjoyed as a pleasurable aesthetic experience, and the desire that there should be maximum opportunity in a university setting for contact by scientist and art student alike. If such a building could be a meeting place and the gallery could provide a shortcut to academic areas, then so much the better. Beyond these guidelines, the program itself did not exist, and the first joint design exercise was to develop a schedule appropriate to such a project, which, as far as we were aware, did not have a social precedent elsewhere.

The site location was determined by the philosophy behind the project and by research into the university background. The latter was traced from its original green fields through and beyond the masterplan and buildings designed by Sir Denys Lasdun. Future growth was indicated along the lines of the Yare valley, and in anticipation of this, a network of roads, drainage, and utilities had already been provided. Respecting

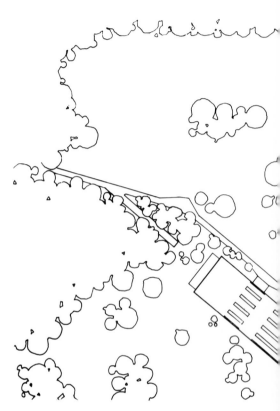

the valley and setting the stage for the next increment of university growth, it was both logical and economical to literally plug into these existing routes with an overhead bridge to link the existing pedestrian spine directly with the new complex. In the spirit of opening up new opportunities for the enjoyment of art on a broader front and opposed to developing an arts ghetto at the opposite end of the campus, the location next to the scientists was ideal. Another important factor in favor of this area was the potential to relate sculpture to a landscape with fine uninterrupted views to the south and west.

During the initial period a wide variety of existing galleries were researched from the viewpoint of visitors and curators alike, providing a number of broad conclusions which strongly influenced the design of the building. These could be summarized as an awareness of the positive qualities of adjustable natural top lighting, the importance

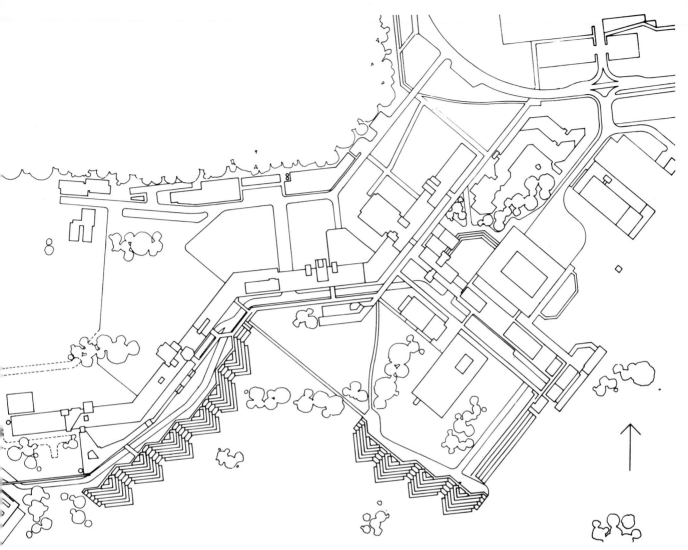

The university masterplan and the Yare Valley were important considerations in the choice of the site for the Sainsbury Center (lower left).

of flexibility for change and growth, the need for good security which was not labor intensive, the value of usable storage space (most museums seemed to have as many works of art inaccessibly closeted away as on display), the need to service a gallery without disturbing either exhibits or users (when changing and adjusting lamps and air filters, for example), a desire to respect and integrate social elements, and a need to see the display and furniture as totally coordinated elements of the overall design.

A wide range of building forms were explored to house the activities—the gallery, senior common room, restaurant, and school—culminating in a design which grouped all the functions under one roof, or umbrella, rather than creating a complex of separate buildings for disparate activities. The result is a linear strip which responds to the line of the valley contours and the geometry of Denys Lasdun's original master plan. The close

physical proximity of normally quite separate activities (galleries are usually confined to viewing and schools to teaching) offers the benefit of cross-fertilization in the spirit of the original program. A system of internal screens, mezzanines, and conservatory courts provides security, privacy, and social focus as appropriate. In such a plan the gallery also becomes the interior route or shortcut to the school, restaurant, and senior common room.

The system of supporting structure and related panels enclosing the roof and walls was developed especially for the project. There are three types of panels: glass, solid aluminum, and grilled aluminum, which are interchangeable by merely undoing six bolts. Here for the first time in a building any part of the roof or walls can be changed easily in about five minutes from solid to glass or vice-versa. This permits a nearly infinite variety of permutations for whatever displays

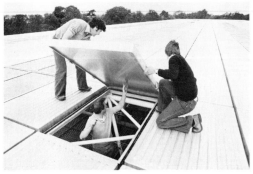

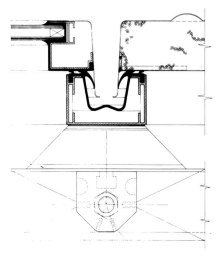

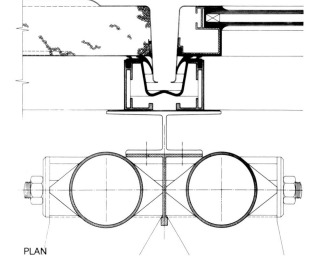

Opposite page: All the panels that clad the Sainsbury Center are interchangeable.

Top, left: This is the first time interchangeable roof panels derived from the automotive and container industries were used in a building.

Top, right: It takes but six bolts to install a panel.

Middle: The three types of panels can be changed in about five minutes.

Bottom: The panels are sealed with neoprene gaskets which do double duty as rainwater channels. They eliminate the need for traditional gutters and downspouts, as can be seen in these cladding panel-to-panel joint details.

SECTION

PLAN

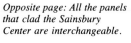

might be required in the future. In a similar manner the exterior entrances can be popped out and shuffled to new locations if desired.

The panels themselves are also interesting technically: they are a sandwich construction with a molded outer skin of anodised aluminum. This is the first application in the building industry of superplastic aluminum. The process by which it was manufactured enables the metal to be molded in a manner normally associated with the plastics industry. In addition the foam-filled sandwich panel has an exceptionally high insulation value, which is an important part of the scheme's low-energy concept. Its highly reflective exterior finish also deflects heat and helps keep the interior cool. The individual panels are sealed with neoprene gaskets, which also double up as rainwater channels, thus eliminating the use of traditional gutters and downspouts. Instead, the entire roof drainage is handled by the grillage in the ground at the base of the building.

The structure of welded steel tubing, freely expressed at the ends, spans 110 feet (33 meters) to form a column-free, unencumbered space for all activities. The clear height of 25 feet (7.5 meters) was determined by the maximum size of works of art, scope for additional levels, and environmental control. The open-ended form allows views through the length of the building to the lake at one end and the woods at the other. The end glass walls were designed for minimum visual interruption, with full-height panels of glass joined only by clear adhesive, as a next step beyond the Willis Faber glass curtain.

The structural members are contained between an inner skin of wall and roof lining and the outer panels, creating a uniform 8-foot (2.4-meter) zone in the wall and roof plane to accommodate a wide variety of functions (such as toilets, darkroom, storage, and mechanical facilities) more fixed than the flexible main areas which they enclose and serve. All circulation spaces and access to them, whether for public and academic use or maintenance, can take place in isolation from the main gallery and university areas. The space in the roof zone enables the lighting to be maintained and focused without disturbing the display below. The inner skin or lining consists of adjustable perforated aluminum louvers with additional motorized banks under the glazed areas. These, combined with the interchangeable exterior panels and a highly flexible system of electric display lighting, produce almost infinitely adjustable light control.

The building was essentially factory produced; the work on site was virtually confined to the process of assembling prefabricated elements.

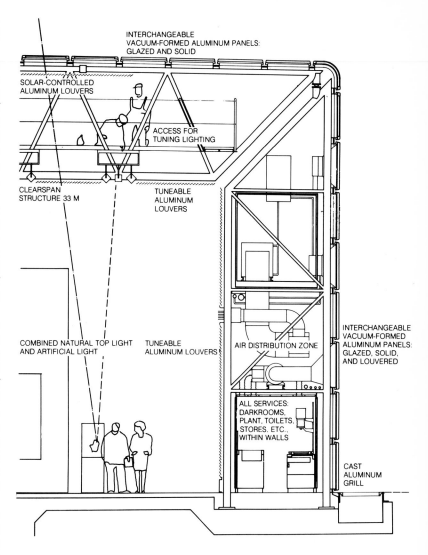

INTERCHANGEABLE VACUUM-FORMED ALUMINUM PANELS: GLAZED AND SOLID

SOLAR-CONTROLLED ALUMINUM LOUVERS

ACCESS FOR TUNING LIGHTING

CLEARSPAN STRUCTURE 33 M

TUNEABLE ALUMINUM LOUVERS

COMBINED NATURAL TOP LIGHT AND ARTIFICIAL LIGHT

TUNEABLE ALUMINUM LOUVERS

AIR DISTRIBUTION ZONE

INTERCHANGEABLE VACUUM-FORMED ALUMINUM PANELS: GLAZED, SOLID, AND LOUVERED

ALL SERVICES: DARKROOMS, PLANT, TOILETS, STORES. ETC., WITHIN WALLS

CAST ALUMINUM GRILL

Opposite page, top: Some functions in the Sainsbury Center like the air-handling units here are more fixed in nature than the main spaces they serve, which prompted us to generate a servant zone to wrap around the tube.

Opposite page, bottom: The Sainsburys wanted the gallery to be rather like their living room where people could sit in easy chairs and read books and magazines. Since their living room was neither air conditioned nor windowless and the collection had been there 40 years in perfectly good condition, they didn't want the gallery to be a hermetically sealed air conditioned environment. Furthermore, the paintings were all conceived in rooms with side or top lighting and the primitive sculptures were created outdoors; our approach would allow the work to be viewed in conditions similar to those of its creation.

Above: Because of the service band, the catwalk system permits workmen to adjust the lighting without closing the gallery or significantly disturbing viewers.

This is in the mainstream of previous projects and is rooted as much in a sense of appropriateness to the age as in cost control, time available, and present-day realities of quality control.

Technology is viewed not as an end in itself, but rather as the means to achieve social goals and open up wider design possibilities. The concept that high technology can be equated with low energy is particularly relevant at this time. In this instance the design of the spaces (their height and shape) and the nature of the enclosing wall (its double thickness, reflectivity, insulation value) combine with the engineering of air movements to attempt an alternative to air conditioning, with its high installation and running costs. The absence of air conditioning is also in the spirit of a living room environment rather than a climate-controlled vault for art works. Despite an extremely hot summer, this has worked well, with the temperature remaining in the 70s.

The idea with technology is to use it appropriately. There are situations where it is best to build in a highly labor-intensive manner (in the Third World, for instance): other times, like here, the reverse is true.

We are currently engaged in projects ranging from large-scale urban planning to experimental housing systems. The technologies that we now consider most relevant stem from the aerospace industries, and it seems no coincidence that events such as the Farnborough Air Show, with its vast array of subcontractors and exhibits, provide more hard-edged clues and inspiration than this year's *Sweet's Catalog*. The technology for our own house project, for instance, is totally rooted in the alloys, glues, and high-strength fixings of the aircraft industry.

Other influences and acknowledgments range from Victorian engineering (where is today's equivalent of the Crystal Palace?) to such apparently misunderstood pioneers as Fuller, Wachsmann, and Eames. Surely there were more roots to 20th-century architecture than some present cul-de-sacs with Disney-like versions of the so-called vernacular, which are as much an affront to any true vernacular as they are to Disneyland.

Our design philosophy could thus be expressed as a process which resolves and integrates those views and polarities which might otherwise be in conflict. Another part of the approach is and always has been a conscious and deliberate attempt to put all those dry objective pieces of the jigsaw (research, statistics, cost schedule, site analysis, structural options—the checklist is endless) together with some very subjective joy—a kind of celebration! That is what architecture should be about.

The unbroken 24-foot (7.3-meter) high single sheets of glass in the Sainsbury Center are a further refinement of the glass technology in the Willis Faber curtain wall.

PHOTOGRAPHY CREDITS

All the photographs and drawings in this book are credited to the individual architects, with the exception of the following: